THE LIBRARY OF AFRICAN-AMERICAN BIOGRAPHY

John David Smith, editor

Richard Wright

Richard Wright

FROM BLACK BOY TO WORLD CITIZEN

Jennifer Jensen Wallach

The Library of
African-American Biography

IVAN R. DEE · CHICAGO

RICHARD WRIGHT. Copyright © 2010 by Jennifer Jensen Wallach.
All rights reserved, including the right to reproduce this book or portions
thereof in any form. For information, address: Ivan R. Dee, Publisher,
1332 North Halsted Street, Chicago 60642, a member of the Rowman
& Littlefield Publishing Group. Manufactured in the United States of
America and printed on acid-free paper.

www.ivanrdee.com

Photographs from the Beinecke Library are reproduced with the special
permission of The Estate of Richard Wright and John Hawkins &
Associates.

Library of Congress Cataloging-in-Publication Data:
Wallach, Jennifer Jensen, 1974–
  Richard Wright : from Black boy to world citizen / Jennifer Jensen
Wallach.
    p. cm.
  Includes index.
  ISBN 978-1-56663-824-1 (cloth : alk. paper)
  1. Wright, Richard, 1908–1960. 2. Authors, American—20th century—
Biography. 3. African American authors—Biography. I. Title.
  PS3545.R815Z895 2010
  813'.52—dc22
  [B]   2009047601

For Charles

Contents

Richard Wright

Prologue

VISITORS from around the world find their way to the Père-Lachaise cemetery to run their fingers across a black marble plaque with the simple chiseled inscription: Richard Wright 1908–1960. They come after navigating the Paris Metro, finding their way from the center of the city, where tourists flock, to the periphery of neighborhoods that radiate in a spiral outward, ending in the Twentieth Arrondissement, home to a bustling Chinatown and to this famous resting place. The quarter surrounding Père-Lachaise has welcomed successive waves of immigrants who, like Wright, came to Paris with the hope of finding freedom and opportunity there that had been denied them in their native lands.

Wright is in good company here, resting alongside artistic luminaries from Edith Piaf to Molière. The walled cemetery contains more than a hundred tree-covered acres, crisscrossed by narrow streets that guide visitors to splendid, artistically wrought shrines. They will find a startling contrast between the modesty of the marker commemorating Richard Wright and the impressive monuments built for so many others. The massive art deco sculpture adorning Oscar Wilde's grave is made still more fascinating by the fact that it is continually covered and recovered with the lipstick kisses of Wilde's admirers. In contrast, Wright's physical imprint on the cemetery is small. For those who know his story, however, the simple marker bearing Wright's name has a quiet assertiveness. It is a solemn testament to the remarkable fact that he rests there at all, so far—both geographically and figuratively—from his origins in rural Mississippi.

After Richard Wright's premature death from a sudden heart attack on November 28, 1960, his body was cremated and his ashes deposited in the large stone columbarium at Père-Lachaise. The flames that consumed Wright's body also devoured a first edition of his 1945 autobiographical account of life in the segregated South, *Black Boy*, placed in his lifeless arms by his wife Ellen. The decision to bury Wright with his masterpiece is a reflection of the fact that regardless of how far he had traveled, Wright's identity remained imprinted by his Southern origins, by the story told so movingly in his most famous work. When he died, Wright was a world-famous writer and a resident of one of the most cosmopolitan cities in the world, but the painful impressions of his deprived childhood had never left him, regardless of how far he traveled.

Wright spent his life trying to escape from the sense of oppression that he first felt as a child in Mississippi. As a teenager he fled from his virulently racist native state to Memphis, where Southern racism was somewhat softened by the greater anonymity of city life. From there he traveled onward to Chicago. While living in the slums of the South Side, he learned how intertwined racial and class oppressions could be. Seeking greater freedom and more professional opportunities, he later moved to New York where he became a wildly successful writer. His brutal first novel, *Native Son* (1940), and his frank autobiography, *Black Boy* (1945), earned him not only fame and critical acclaim but also the money he needed to continue his search for freedom. After a decade in New York, Wright and his family relocated to Paris in 1947. Wright was thrilled to find himself in a more racially tolerant climate. He thought he was finally positioned to shed the emotional baggage of his deprived Southern childhood.

But even Paris, his chosen city, did not prove to be his utopia. He traveled widely in Europe, Africa, and Asia but never found a place where he could feel completely at peace. Shortly before his death, he contemplated moving to London, looking until the end for an environment that would ease what was at root an internal problem. Changing his locale could not relieve him from a persistent sense of psychological tension. The world of his imagination provided him with his only escape, writing his only reprieve from his tangled and restless thoughts. Despite his prolific output of nearly a dozen books published during his life and hundreds of unpublished manuscript pages that he left behind, his work soothed him only temporarily. It could not provide a cure for his permanent state of agitation.

Wright enjoyed many of the perquisites that came with fame and financial security, but he never allowed himself to forget his origins. He felt a lifelong sense of obligation to be a spokesperson for those who had neither his means nor his access to the reading public. Although he took the craft of writing seriously, he found the idea of art for its own sake abhorrent. When he wrote he did so in the hope of making a social difference. He saw words as not merely ornamental; they were instead powerful weapons, weapons that he, as a man of conscience who had been born with certain talents, was obliged to use on behalf of others.

Throughout African-American history, many talented, prosperous, or educated individuals have felt this same sense of duty to become race men or race women, to represent in thought and deed those less fortunate. But appointing oneself as a representative is an act that is always fraught with ambiguities. The accident of his birth gave Wright a greater feeling of social obligation than he may otherwise have felt. He would never be seen merely as a writer or an intellectual, but as a *black* writer, a *black* intellectual. With that label came certain responsibilities, which he met to the best of his ability. Yet he often longed for the anonymity that came with white privilege, the carefree ability to speak only for oneself. Wright did not always understand the people he tried to represent, nor did he always like them. His ideas were often idiosyncratic, and he was seldom swayed by majority opinion.

At root, Wright was an individualist. He once wrote in his journal that the overwhelming question in his life was "How can I live freely?" He was to discover that globetrotting provided an insufficient answer to that question. Furthermore his political and intellectual journeys—ranging from Marxism to existentialism to Pan-Africanism—similarly failed to yield the sense of liberation he craved. When he embraced ideas, he did so boldly. His confident, if not brazen, prose style made his work powerful, but his certitude could be somewhat blinding. He often failed to understand other points of view or to gauge effectively the way his own ideas would be received. He was not intellectually intransigent; he could and frequently did change his mind about things. But he did so at the urging of his own inner voice, not in reaction to the murmuring of his critics.

Upon meeting thirty-three-year-old Richard Wright in 1941, the renowned sociologist Robert Park famously demanded to know of the young writer, "How in hell did you happen?" The causes of Park's amazement are clear. Nothing in Wright's deprived background could have foretold his astronomical success. As unique as he was, however, Wright must also be interpreted within the context of his milieu. Although he was certainly singular in terms of his talent, he did not walk through history unaccompanied. His story of poverty in the rural South was shared by millions. Many from similar backgrounds also fled from the South in search of greater opportunity. Upon Wright's arrival in New York, he discovered a thriving network of African-American writers and activists already well established. Even in Europe, Wright found that he was hardly the only African-American artist with the means or imagination to seek a new life there. At every new destination he discovered that his journey had not been solitary.

The biography of Richard Wright that follows examines his life through the twin prisms of his peculiarity and his typicality, assessing his unusual success in the historical context that helped create him. This account of Wright's life describes not only the various physical environments that he lived in during his short but full life, it also seeks to understand the geography of his interior world.

CHAPTER ONE

Black Boy

෨ Richard Nathaniel Wright was born into poverty on September 4, 1908, in a crude log cabin near the hamlet of Roxie, Mississippi. He later described his birthplace as being "too far back in the woods to hear the train whistle," a place where you could "only hear the hoot owls holler." His parents, Nathaniel Wright and Ella Wilson Wright, were the children of slaves. At the time of Richard's birth, the couple was eking out an existence as sharecroppers on land not far from where their parents had involuntarily labored. Wright's harsh Mississippi childhood was colored by both the dark history of slavery and the failed promises of emancipation.

After the Civil War ended, the freedpeople, including Wright's grandparents, were faced with overwhelming odds as they struggled to build new lives for themselves with few resources and little assistance. Still, few would have traded the uncertainties of freedom for the all-too-certain future posed by the prison of slavery. Wright's grandfathers on both sides of the family made their disdain for slavery well known by seizing on the opportunity offered by the Civil War to fight for their freedom in what was to become a war of liberation. When Natchez was occupied by the Union Army in July 1863, Wright's paternal grandfather, Nathaniel Wright, fled Rucker's Plantation where he was a field laborer to join the Fifty-eighth U.S. Colored Infantry. In 1865 his maternal grandfather, Richard Wilson, also escaped from the fields in order to fight, making his way to Cairo, Illinois, where he enlisted in the Union Navy and served for the last three months of the conflict.

When the war ended, both Nathaniel Wright and Richard Wilson had reason to feel initially hopeful about their prospects as freedpeople. Nathaniel managed to become the owner of a piece of land that he had worked on as a slave, a remarkable feat that surely made him the envy of his neighbors. Richard too made his way home to Mississippi where he participated enthusiastically in the experiment of interracial democracy that characterized the Reconstruction period after the war. During this all too brief historical moment, black men were enfranchised. Many took part earnestly in the political process by exercising their rights at the ballot box and even by holding elective office. Hiram Revels, the first black to be elected to serve in the U.S. Senate, and Blanche Bruce, the first African American to serve a full term in that body, were both elected in Wright's native Mississippi. Richard Wilson played a proud role in the electoral process, serving as an armed guard at the ballot boxes, doing his part to make sure that black voting rights were respected.

This quick and remarkable transformation from slave to citizen gave Richard Wilson ample cause for optimism about the future when he proposed to eighteen-year-old Margaret Bolden in 1871. "Maggie" was slight and attractive with piercing brown eyes and long straight dark hair. Her fair complexion testified to a racially mixed ancestry. She could easily have passed for white, a fact that her grandson Richard later found puzzling as he tutored himself on the complicated subject of Southern race relations. The young couple settled in Natchez, Mississippi, where Maggie worked as a midwife while her husband found employment as a farm laborer. Although illiterate, through hard work, tenacity, and some luck they earned a precarious place in the burgeoning black middle class. Due to the overwhelming poverty of the region's black inhabitants, holding a middling economic station did not mean that the family lived in comfort but rather that they were at least marginally better off than the landless black peasantry in the countryside. The Wilsons were prosperous enough to purchase a home and to make certain that each of their nine children received some degree of education. Several, including Wright's mother Ella, who was born in 1883, acquired enough rudimentary schooling to work as schoolteachers.

As the Wilsons struggled to hold on to their modest material gains, it grew clearer that the progressive promises of Reconstruction would not ultimately bear fruit. Paramilitary groups like the Ku Klux Klan terrorized blacks, driving them away from the ballot box through a campaign of systematic, ruthless violence. Hundreds of black Mississippians lost their lives at the hands of angry whites for attempting to exercise their right to vote or for trying to enjoy too enthusiastically the fruits of their newfound freedom. By 1875 it was clear that Mississippi's brief experiment in interracial democracy would fail.

Due to Richard Wilson's unfortunately frail health, the family's financial position deteriorated along with their civil rights. Because he was at times bedridden, Richard's ability to contribute to the family's income grew unsteady. The combination of his ill health and his political disappointments turned him into the understandably bitter and broken old man that his grandson was to write about decades later in *Black Boy*. As Richard and Maggie Wilson's family economy plummeted, they left their large wooden house in Natchez and moved to the capital city of Jackson to be nearer to their son Clark, who bought them a modest house at 1107 Lynch

Street. Young Richard Wright was ultimately to spend much of his childhood living in this home. It was in this setting that he learned about the bitter disappointments of emancipation as he watched his grandfather fight to receive the pension due him as a Civil War veteran.

When Richard Wilson enlisted in the Union Navy, his name had been mistakenly recorded as "Richard Vincent," and the Bureau of Pensions continuously used the name discrepancy to deny him an annuity. Undaunted, the illiterate elderly man dictated letter after letter filled with details about his service—names of comrades and descriptions of fighting—hoping to stumble upon just the right piece of evidence to convince officials of his claim. Despite the tenacity of his letter-writing campaign and his unwillingness to accept meekly the latest in a lifelong series of injustices, the old man was reluctant to share the particulars of either his service or his battle to secure a pension with his curious young grandson. Wright later recalled that he "never heard him speak of white people; I think he hated them too much to talk of them."

In spite of Richard Wilson's reluctance to satisfy his grandson's curiosity, young Wright managed to glean the outline of the story from other relatives who told him just enough so that he could construct a link between his family's own present-day difficulties and the mysterious past of slavery. The experience of his grandfather provided a sobering lesson about the grim realities of past as well as present, giving young Wright clues about the historical baggage he had inherited and about the likelihood of his being able to cast off those burdens. Richard Wilson's campaign for justice, which began during the days of his bondage and continued in armed conflict in both the Civil War and as a defender of black liberty during Reconstruction, was anticlimactically transformed into a solitary and unsuccessful struggle against a series of disinterested Washington bureaucrats.

Wright was part of the second generation to be born in freedom. By the time of his birth, the limitations of that freedom had already become perfectly clear. Mired in poverty, barred from the ballot box, and confined to inferior and segregated neighborhoods and public spaces, most rural black Mississippians, like the young Wright family, faced an uphill battle just putting together the economic rudiments of survival. Most of the region's black citizens, like Ella and Nathaniel Wright, worked as sharecroppers, farming land they did not own in return for a share of the crop value.

Sharecroppers depended not only upon the whims of the landlord but also on prices at the cotton exchange and the weather, factors that neither owner nor tenant could control. It was nearly impossible to prosper even under the best of circumstances, and many sharecroppers lived in worse houses and ate less nutritious diets than their enslaved ancestors had. Most African-American families teetered on the edge of economic disaster. The Wrights discovered they could no longer survive in the countryside after Ella gave birth to another son, Leon Alan, in 1910. With two young children to care for, Ella could spend little time working in the fields, persuading the young couple that they could not derive a decent living from the land. Thus Wright made what was to be a permanent escape from rural life at a young age, spending the rest of his childhood in a series of Southern towns. Leaving the countryside while still a toddler, he retained his plantation origins as family lore rather than as concrete memory.

In retrospect Wright learned to appreciate the relative advantages of growing up in the South's fledgling urban centers. At the age of fourteen, while living at his grandparents' home in Jackson, he was to take a temporary job as a secretary to an illiterate black insurance salesman who solicited poor Delta blacks. Richard traveled to the countryside to fill out insurance forms, along the way catching a glimpse of the fate he had escaped. As he slept in crude wooden shacks and dined on fatback and black-eyed peas, he was repelled by what he described as the "bare, bleak pool of black life." He had to remind himself that he too had been born on a plantation.

On one level he felt separated from, if not superior to, the seemingly simpleminded inhabitants of the countryside. He felt worldly and well educated in comparison. On the other hand he felt deeply and profoundly connected to this experience because, like it or not, he realized he was a part of the historical processes that had created this bleak environment. Later he captured his personal feeling of connection to black rural poverty in *12 Million Black Voices* (1941), a photo essay that combined his prose with a series of gripping photographs of African-American life taken by photographers during the New Deal. The text refers movingly to "our black bodies" as the "tools" that kept the plantation system running. With the use of the inclusive pronoun, Wright revealed his inability ever to transcend completely— despite his best efforts—those plantation origins.

When the Wright family fled from the countryside in 1911, they, like many of their contemporaries, hoped that relocation to an urban center might better their fortunes. Nearby Memphis, known to some as the "capital" of the Mississippi Delta, seemed to be a logical choice for their new home. They made their journey by water, traveling up the Mississippi River from Natchez to Memphis on the *Kate Adams*, an old-fashioned steamboat. From the very beginning, the journey was a disappointment to Wright, who soon discovered that the dingy vessel hardly resembled the impressive ship he had designed in his imagination.

Memphis, then a city of about a hundred thousand inhabitants, also ultimately failed to meet the family's expectations. The Wrights lived just south of Beale Street, which due to the pioneering efforts of musicians like Frank Stokes and Memphis Minnie was about to become the center of a vibrant black blues scene. The famous Memphis blues were largely guitar based, but many musicians also played homemade instruments, like jugs and washboards. These innovations gave the music a unique sound while also reflecting the poverty of performers who could not afford store-bought instruments. Many of the musicians who made Beale Street famous had, like the Wright family, traveled from the countryside to the city in search of economic opportunity, and they documented their hardships in soulful lyrics. Soon the Wrights would be able to identify strongly with Furry Lewis's lament, "So much trouble floating in the air."

For the time being, Nathaniel Wright was fortunate to find work quickly as a night porter in a Beale Street drugstore. Nonetheless the family discovered some immediate disadvantages of city life. Cramped into a one-room tenement apartment, they missed the spaciousness of rural living. The small concrete courtyard in front of their apartment made the children long for the green spaces they had enjoyed in Mississippi. Nathaniel worked nights and slept during the day, a situation that made their confined surroundings seem that much more restrictive. Richard began to fear his father, who responded to the tensions of urban living by ruling over the flat tyrannically, complaining about everything from Ella's cooking to the noise the children made while playing.

One day Nathaniel complained about a mewing kitten, gruffly ordering Richard to "kill it." Richard, to his little brother Leon's horror, took his father's edict literally and strangled the tiny creature. Wright later came to regret redirecting his aggression toward his father at the kitten, particularly when Ella made him bury it after the sun went down, darkly hinting to Richard that God might not show him more mercy than he had shown the kitten. Wright recounted this gruesome episode in *Black Boy* not only to reveal his growing resentment of his gruff father but to demonstrate what he saw as the brutalizing impact of a harsh environment. In his mind there was nothing fundamentally flawed in his nature that enabled him to kill the kitten. Instead he felt driven to that cruel action by poverty, poor living conditions, and a tense family life.

Pressures at home drove Nathaniel away more and more frequently, and he soon come to prefer the allure of Beale Street and other women to the company of his wife and children. Eventually he stopped coming home altogether. Initially Richard reveled in the newfound freedom offered by his father's absence, but his sentiments changed when the money ran out, and he soon came to associate his father's absence with the hunger pains that now afflicted him. Ella found a job working as a cook for a white family, and for a time she managed to support her children on her meager wages. She told Richard that, as a fatherless child, he would have to take on additional responsibilities, including caring for his younger brother and shopping for the family's food, tasks he gravely assumed. But he also took advantage of his mother's absences to explore other aspects of his new environment. He found himself lingering in saloons, and he remembered drinking alcohol provided by bemused patrons who also paid the little boy to repeat bawdy sayings for their amusement.

Richard was able to expand upon the crude education provided by the city streets beginning in 1915 when he entered school at the Howe Institute, a small private school for black children in his neighborhood. Despite her economic difficulties, Ella, like her parents before her, seemed determined to make sure that her sons received an education. That same year the struggling mother took her estranged husband to court, suing him for child support. Nathaniel, however, shamelessly played on the white judge's stereotype of black incompetence and childishness. Grinning, he assured the judge that he was already doing all that he could for his children. The judge was unmoved by Ella's desperation and declined to issue a court order mandating support.

The family's humiliation in court gave way to a graver situation when Ella became suddenly ill and unable to work. Under these pressing circumstances she made the extraordinarily difficult decision to place both of her sons in an orphanage temporarily. Thus in quick succession the young Wright brothers had been deserted by both their parents. In addition to the emotional trauma of abandonment, they suffered from the physical consequences of hunger and malnourishment. At the orphanage they were fed just two skimpy meals each day. They spent their time tormented by hunger, working at mindless tasks like picking the grass lawn, which the orphanage could not afford to have mowed. In despair, Wright began what was to become a pattern of behavior in his life, his strategy for dealing with frustration: he fled. A white policemen found him wandering around a strange neighborhood and returned him. Soon Ella rescued her sons, arriving at the orphanage with news that she planned to rebuild the family's life in Elaine, Arkansas, where her favorite sister, Maggie, lived. Choosing a reverse migration, she hoped the small town would prove to be a less hostile environment than the big city. First, however, she would take the boys to visit their grandparents in Jackson.

Their trip there in 1916 proved to be transformational for Wright. While in Jackson he discovered the twin concerns that would guide him for the rest of his life—an interest in creative writing and a desire to understand both the ideology and practice of racism. In order to help make ends meet, Granny and Grandpa had taken in a boarder, a young schoolteacher also named Ella. One day Wright encountered her sitting on the front porch reading *Bluebeard and His Seven Wives,* and he begged her to tell him about it. This seemingly innocent request was complicated by Granny's stern Seventh Day Adventist faith, which made her leery of any influences that she deemed to be ungodly. Unfortunately for her grandson, in Granny's mind fiction fit the category of "the Devil's work" because it consisted of what she unambiguously labeled "lies." In spite of her tenuous position in the household, the young schoolteacher's sympathy for the boy's curiosity outweighed her fear of losing her accommodations, and she began quietly and dramatically to narrate the bloody story.

Richard was transfixed by this medium that offered him an imaginative entrance to another world, an escape from the unsavory aspects of the one he knew. From this point onward, storytelling was to be his escape. Reading and writing were to expand his mental horizons and save him from being crushed under the weight of an oppressive environment. Later, after he managed to make a living as a writer, his prose would provide the literal means for flight, affording him the funds to leave the United States altogether. In retrospect he realized that this encounter with *Bluebeard* constituted the "first experience in my life that had elicited . . . a total emotional response." He recalled, "I had tasted to me what was life, and I would have more of it, somehow, someway." Ella's tutelage about the life of the mind was, however, short-lived. She was soon interrupted by a screeching Granny who brought the tale to an abrupt and partial conclusion, slapping Richard across the face when he protested.

Although Wright had endured hunger and abandonment and had wandered the city streets of Memphis on his own, these deprivations paled in comparison to Granny's unwillingness to let him enjoy this delight of storytelling, something that even the poorest family could afford in abundance. With her unyielding religious certainty, Granny tried to cut her grandson off from the one thing he instinctively knew could save him from the bleak circumstances of racism and poverty. He was embittered by her attempts to control even his thoughts. Secretly he also resented his frail mother for not standing up for him, for not sensing what he so desperately needed.

Nonetheless the effects of the whispered story fragment were irreversible; thus inspired, an intellectually awakened Wright now began to try assembling a more cohesive understanding of his social world. The most befuddling issue for him was race. This initial stirring of racial consciousness was of curiosity and not of pain as he tried to puzzle out the intricacies of segregation and the mystery of Granny's light-colored skin. He soon noticed that his mother expressed irritation when he quizzed her on these subjects. No doubt Ella Wright, like African Americans throughout history, was reluctant to see her child lose his innocence and to begin to realize what a tyrant Jim Crow could be. But her attempts to shield him from the grim realities of the Southern caste system proved futile. After the young family left Jackson for their trip to Elaine, they had to face head-on the horrific implications of Southern racism.

Richard and Leon were thrilled at the prospect of going to live with their favorite aunt and her husband who owned a trim bungalow in the Mississippi Delta town of Elaine,

Arkansas. Their uncle, Silas Hoskins, owned a successful tavern, which served blacks who worked in the region's thriving lumber trade. Because business was good, the Hoskinses' table was laden with food at every meal. Hunger had haunted the Wright boys after their father abandoned them and again at the orphanage and even at their grandparents' home, where the Wilsons' meager resources could not be adequately stretched to meet the nutritional needs of two active boys. Now, for the first time in memory, Richard was faced with abundance. He gorged himself at mealtimes and could not be broken of the habit of filling his pockets with dinner rolls, his attempt to stave off future hunger should he again be faced with scarcity. Richard's limited life experience had already demonstrated that the future was unpredictable, that fate was cruel, and that it was up to the individual to plan for future disasters.

As it turned out, Richard's fear that this life of relative abundance would not last was prescient. Uncle Hoskins kept a revolver next to his bed, and the weapon's implicit intimation that danger lurked on the fringes of their cozy life was not lost on Richard. One day Uncle Hoskins did not return from his saloon, and the family had to wait several hours before hearing the news, delivered by a young black messenger boy: Hoskins was dead. He had been shot by local white men who, it was later discovered, were jealous of his economic success. He had ignored repeated warnings to stop living so well and to abandon his business to white interests or leave town.

Young Richard was permanently traumatized by Hoskins's lynch murder. In the aftermath, though he had not personally suffered any unpleasant encounters with whites, his anxiety was such that Wright felt as though he had "been the victim of a thousand lynchings." From this point onward he lived in a state of tension and dread, certain that the hostile white world could crush him like it had his uncle if he failed to live by its arbitrary rules.

The Wilson sisters decided to flee town at once for fear they too might be killed. In their haste to leave Elaine, they took only their household belongings. Aunt Maggie never saw her husband's body, and she did not dare attempt to claim any of his economic assets. The sisters' instincts to flee rather than fight for justice ensured the family's survival, and their lack of faith in the fair-mindedness of the local white community ultimately proved well founded. A few short years later, in 1919, a group of African-American sharecroppers from Elaine and surrounding Philips County banded together to form a labor union. Not only were local whites unwilling to bargain collectively, but rumors began to spread that local blacks were planning an insurrection. In response, hundreds of armed whites swarmed into Elaine from surrounding areas, killing as many as several hundred black people and arresting hundreds more. In the hostile racial climate of Elaine, ambitious and assertive African Americans like Uncle Hoskins did not stand a chance.

After fleeing their home, Ellen and Maggie settled in nearby West Helena, Arkansas. Together they supported Richard and Leon by working as cooks in white homes. Their standard of living deteriorated considerably from their days in the Elaine bungalow, and they lived in a series of squalid rental properties. At one point they lived next door to a house of prostitution, a situation that provided the Wright brothers with a crude and bewildering crash course in sex education. At another address the children's chief source of entertainment consisted of designing homemade boats out of garbage, which they floated down the sewage ditch outside their home.

Much to Richard's chagrin, the precarious new life the family had built was soon disrupted when Aunt Maggie became embroiled in another racial drama. Her lover, "Professor Matthews," was wanted by the police after a mysterious conflict involving local whites. To avoid the possibility of arrest or another lynching, the couple decided to flee northward in the middle of the night. Once again Ella was left as the sole supporter of her two sons, who soon suffered from the all too familiar pangs of not having enough to eat.

Young Wright was so hungry that one day he decided to sell his toy poodle, Betsy, for a dollar to buy food. He ventured into a white neighborhood with the freshly bathed white dog in his arms, summoning up the courage to knock on several doors. Although he was generally rebuffed, one young woman squealed upon seeing the little dog and gathered together ninety-seven cents toward the purchase price, promising to give Richard the remainder later. But the boy was suddenly overcome with anxiety and anger as he realized how much material comfort the people in the white neighborhood enjoyed while he and his family had not even enough to eat. He knew that the white people who lived in luxury while others did without were responsible for much of the suffering in the black community, including, of course, the death of Uncle Hoskins and the disappearance of Aunt Maggie and Professor Matthews. A mixture of pride and fear temporarily silenced his hunger pains, and he refused to part with his pet. Betsy was crushed by a coal wagon a few days later, providing Richard another lesson about his powerlessness to control his environment.

Soon after that incident, Ella suffered a stroke that left her partially paralyzed and temporarily unable to communicate with her terrified children. Granny struggled to find enough money to transport the family to Jackson. Like other poor families when tragedy hit, the Wilsons pooled resources to provide medical care for Ella and support for her sons. Wright received further tutelage on the nature of

Jim Crow realities when his mother was taken to a hospital for surgery. A white specialist agreed to perform an experimental operation, but due to the primitive nature of medical facilities available for black residents of Mississippi, the procedure could be performed only at the segregated white hospital. Wright's mother was bandaged from head to toe, and thus disguised she was briefly admitted. After surgery she was immediately discharged and returned home via a stretcher placed in a baggage car on a train. But the rushed surgery performed under such humiliating circumstances failed to accomplish the intended miracle. Ella never fully recovered her health and was never again able to support her two sons.

Granny and Grandpa Wilson agreed to look after their ailing daughter, but they did not have the resources to take in Richard and Leon too. Leon, it was decided, would travel north to live with his Aunt Maggie who was now settled in Detroit. Richard was to stay nearby in Greenwood with his Uncle Clark and his wife Jody. The couple lived in a tidy, comfortable home. There Richard would have enough to eat and could attend school. During his stay in their home, however, he inadvertently discovered that a young boy had died in his bed, and he became terrified at the prospect of being haunted by a ghost. This emotional instability frightened his relatives. He had been traumatized by a lifetime of poverty and uncertainty, compounded by his growing understanding of the cruel nature of Southern racism. He lacked the emotional resources to cope with this strange and new situation. He longed to be with the only person who he felt loved him, the most constant presence in his short but tumultuous life. Finally he was allowed to return to Jackson to be with his mother.

Wright was to live with his grandparents for the next six years. As an uninvited dependent, his position in the home was delicate. He sensed that Granny viewed him chiefly as a financial burden rather than as a beloved grandson. His outsider status was compounded by the fact that he was repelled by Granny's stern Seventh Day Adventist faith. The conflict between grandmother and grandson over the story of Bluebeard proved to be a foreshadowing of the tense relationship that would develop in the years to come. Granny's religion placed prohibitions not only against the reading of fiction but against working on Saturday, the church's Sabbath, and eating pork, that form of cheap protein most widely available to poor Southerners. Richard chafed at these limitations. He continued to read fiction despite Granny's strictures, but the magazines he brought into the home were often wordlessly removed from his bedroom and burned in the kitchen stove. Granny's dietary rules placed additional strain on the already stretched budget of the Wilson household. Members of the family subsisted mainly on gravy made from flour, plus lard and greens, which were never served in abundance and, according to Richard, caused him indigestion. Because Granny would not allow Richard to work on Saturday, he was initially unable to get a part-time job to subsidize his diet, his scanty wardrobe, or the household budget.

Richard's innate religious cynicism set him apart from his devout family who regarded him as a sinner in their midst, scrutinizing his behavior accordingly. He briefly attended a Seventh Day Adventist school taught by his zealous Aunt Addie, who despised what she regarded as Richard's impertinence. Their relationship reached a boiling point when Addie wrongfully accused Richard of eating walnuts in the classroom, a conflict that escalated to the point where Richard confronted his young aunt with a knife. Horrified by his actions, the family launched a campaign for Wright's conversion, forcing him to attend all-night church services and spend daily time in prayer. They even enlisted his peers in

Wright's stern and religious maternal grandmother, Margaret Wilson, had been born
into slavery. Wright, who was intellectually
independent from childhood, frequently
clashed with "Granny." *(Yale Collection of
American Literature, Beinecke Rare Book
and Manuscript Library)*

the cause, but their interest in the fate of his immortal soul
left Richard unmoved.

Increasingly he felt detached and set apart from the family members whose hostility toward him posed a more direct
obstacle to his sense of well-being than the more amorphous
threat of white racism. Later he would realize that the racist
environment of the South had driven Granny to create the
small, hard world of intolerance and rigid religious obser-
vance that she forced the family to inhabit. Because there
was so little she could control in a universe designed to ter-
rorize African Americans and limit their life chances, she

found ways to extract religious meaning from her suffering. All the while she compounded the miseries of her resentful grandson who developed a lifelong hostility toward organized religion. Richard vowed to choose a different strategy for dealing with white oppression when freed from Granny's grip.

It came as an enormous relief to Richard when Granny finally pronounced him irredeemable. In the aftermath of this proclamation, he was finally allowed to leave the religious school and enroll in the local Jim Hill School. Until now he had had but a single uninterrupted year of schooling, and he was placed in the fifth grade, two grades behind his age group. Much to his joy and surprise, his teachers recognized his keen intelligence, and within two weeks he was promoted to the sixth grade.

Among his schoolmates were members of the black middle class and many with middle-class aspirations. In contrast to his more fortunate classmates, Wright lacked the money for proper clothes, textbooks, and, even more fundamentally, food. His pride compelled him to feign indifference during the lunch period each day when his classmates bought sandwiches while his stomach grumbled. His heart was set, however, not just on satisfying his physical hunger and on learning to succeed within the confines of segregation but in finding another way of living altogether.

Wright felt enlivened by the company of his new classmates. His rocky home life had encouraged him to keep his ideas and emotions to himself rather than risk condemnation or ridicule. For the first time he managed to break through his isolation and to forge friendships, some of which were to last for years to come. He cultivated a friendly and outgoing personality designed to mask a nagging feeling of alienation and a habit, born from his tumultuous childhood, of being unable to trust anyone. His ruse worked. He was well liked by his classmates who scarcely understood the depth of their classmate's anger toward his repressive family, his outrage against Southern racism, and his ambition to overcome the limitations posed by both. Internally Wright was torn. He longed for companionship and enjoyed finding a sense of belonging among his school friends, but he also felt set apart by his poverty and his disinterest in striving after the lifestyle of a middle-class black Southerner. Many of his classmates were concerned with using their education to acquire nicer houses, respectable jobs, and eligible mates. Wright's dreams, while equally urgent, were hazier than the material longings of some of his peers.

From a young age Wright felt he was destined to remain a permanent outsider, plagued by what he described as his "eternal difference" from everyone else. Throughout his autobiography he uses the idea of hunger to describe his distinctiveness metaphorically, demonstrating that it was his enormous appetite for experiences and ideas that set him apart from his classmates. During his early days he was, of course, often literally hungry, but he was not sated intellectually either. He could not reconcile himself to life in the segregated South, to the tyranny of his grandmother's religion, or to the intellectual limitations posed by both of these overwhelming obstacles. Although racial oppression united him with other members of the black community, and their shared experiences brought Richard moments of consolation, he sensed that he was destined to tread what he labeled as a "strange and separate road." He yearned for a different way of living, though his limited environment had not yet provided him with enough exposure to discern the precise nature of his longing. Thinking back to his encounter with the Bluebeard story, Wright began to realize that part of his vision for the future was a life filled with books, ideas, and storytelling. Increasingly he began to flirt with the idea that

in addition to reading books, he might also be able to write
them.

Wright's sense of alienation had been fueled by his unstable and unhappy childhood. No doubt it was also the product
of his particular creative genius, which distanced him from
others with more moderate abilities and more pedestrian desires. The fact that he managed to nurture his talents despite
having been born poor and black in segregated Mississippi
was due in large part to another inborn trait: an innate arro-
gance, a certainty that his way of seeing and experiencing the
world was a superior one. This translated into a readiness to
harshly criticize anyone who disagreed with him or failed to
understand him. On many occasions he shocked his friends
and acquaintances—and later his readers—by his audacious
generalizations about entire groups of people. His childhood
community was no exception. Looking back upon his early
years he recalled, "I used to mull over the absence of real
kindness in Negroes, how unstable was our tenderness . . .
how timid our joy, how bare our traditions, how hollow our
memories." Although many other African Americans who
came of age during the era of segregation reported receiving
some consolation from a tightly knit black community and
rich, communal cultural practices, this was not the case for
Wright. He was to find something lacking in every community that he tried to call home throughout his life.

Although the reality of white racial hatred had loomed in
his consciousness at least since the time of Uncle Hoskins's
lynching, by the time Wright enrolled at Jim Hill he had yet
to figure out what kind of relationship he wanted with the
world outside his family or the black community. Whether
due to the chaos of his upbringing or the brooding and emotional solitude of his nature, Wright had clearly failed to
sense some necessary clues for survival in the segregated
South. When at long last Granny relaxed her rule about Sab-

bath work, reasoning perhaps that the reprobate in their midst might at least contribute financially to the household, Richard quickly discovered that he was ill equipped to perform the role of a properly subordinated black employee.

In Mississippi during the early twentieth century, the legal barriers that kept African Americans from being fully incorporated into Southern society were bolstered by an informal set of rules of conduct, which Wright referred to as the "ethics of Jim Crow." These included concrete behaviors for blacks, like remembering to say "sir" or "ma'am," to step out of the way of whites, and to approach white homes via the back door. Other expected norms of black behavior were more amorphous and difficult to perform. Blacks were not supposed to seem too intelligent or ambitious but rather were to appear simpleminded and content. To avoid white disapproval, African Americans were thus expected to assume a ceaselessly cheerful demeanor. For Wright these behaviors did not come naturally but were achieved through years of study and concentration, made more difficult by the fact that potential mistakes could prove deadly. The precariousness of his situation was made clear once again to Wright when he heard the chilling news that an acquaintance had been lynched for violating one of the region's most sacred taboos by allegedly having sex with a white prostitute. If he did not behave as local whites expected, he knew that he too could end up like his friend or his Uncle Hoskins. The stakes could not have been higher.

Richard learned exactly how ill prepared he was to survive in the South during his first job interviews. When he sought employment doing household chores after school and on Saturday, his first potential employer asked him directly whether he was prone to steal. Wright found this line of questioning preposterous since no self-respecting thief would own up to such behavior. His failure to master the peculiar logic of Southern segregation was further revealed during his second job interview when he told his would-be employer that he wished to become a writer, an idea that she found fanciful coming from the mouth of a malnourished black teenager. The proud and intellectually precocious Wright was enraged that he had to subject himself to the humiliation of interviews with potential white employers who viewed him as little more than a trained animal, someone capable of chopping firewood or of milking a cow, but not as a fully sentient being with aspirations beyond the drudgery of servant work.

Because he was inept at understanding white expectations, Wright initially had trouble maintaining steady employment. Although he needed work desperately, he always came across as too inquisitive or not sufficiently deferential. He could remember to perform the scripted part of the simpleminded servant only briefly, then he would "forget and act straight and human again . . . forgetting the artificial status of race and class." His friend Dick Jordan took pity on Wright for his ineptness and schooled him on vital survival skills, teaching him how to please his white employers while hiding his real feelings. Richard was enraged by the need to adopt such demeaning forms of behavior, but he was also motivated by the goal of earning the money that would make possible his escape from the South. He decided that he had to learn to adapt to the Southern caste system, to master its intricacies, so that he could find a way to overcome it. Eventually, if only temporarily, he swallowed his pride and mastered the art of dissembling, learning to behave as if he had little intelligence and even less ambition.

Dick Jordan was not the only friend to help Richard as he refined his plan to leave the South. He was employed for a time by the Wall family, the first friendly whites with whom he had a sustained encounter. He felt so comfortable in their presence that he confided in them and sought their advice as he made his future plans. Thanks to their example, he learned that he need not automatically fear all white people. Although Granny regarded his interest in becoming a writer as a form of blasphemy, Wright was encouraged in his efforts by Malcolm Rogers, editor of the black weekly the *Southern Register*, who published one of Wright's first attempts at fiction, a gothic story that Richard later recalled naming "The Voodoo of Hell's Half-Acre." His teachers also recognized his talent, and he excelled academically. When he graduated from ninth grade at the Smith Robertson School in 1925, he did so as valedictorian.

Like the rest of Richard's life, the graduation ceremony was tainted by the realities of Southern racism. Support among the white community for black education beyond a crude elementary-school level was meager, and the black faculty and administrators who pressed for middle school and high school educational opportunities for black children had to make their case delicately so as not to threaten prevailing white sensibilities. Every move that the students and faculty at Smith Robertson made in the presence of the white authorities who provided their funding was premeditated and carefully choreographed to achieve the desired effect. This included the valedictorian's address. Richard was appalled when the principal, W. H. Lanier, handed him a carefully worded speech that he was expected to deliver at the ceremony. He self-righteously refused to do so, feeling no apparent empathy for the difficulty of Lanier's position. Lanier threatened to deny him his diploma or a recommendation for a teaching position should he refuse to cooperate, but Wright was undeterred. He made a down payment on a suit to wear to graduation, stubbornly read a speech that he wrote himself, and thus ended his formal education.

After graduation Wright decided it was time to leave the South, and he made the difficult decision to resort to dishonest means to make his escape. His earning power at legitimate jobs was meager, and whatever he made disappeared rapidly in the face of overwhelming need in the Wilson home. So in violation of his code of ethics as well as his pragmatic wish to avoid a possible run-in with the Southern legal system, Wright resorted to stealing to finance his journey out of Mississippi. He took a job at a movie theater where he helped his co-workers resell tickets, pocketing a share of the extra money. Even more daringly, he stole a gun from a neighbor and some canned fruit from the warehouse of Jackson College, a nearby black school. He sold these items to build up his hundred-dollar nest egg, the magic number he had settled upon as what he needed to leave home. Having achieved his financial goal, Wright bid his mother goodbye and, like his parents before him, headed to Memphis to begin a new and better life.

CHAPTER TWO

Refugee

ﾟﾞ By the time Richard Wright arrived in Memphis in November 1925, his estranged father Nathaniel Wright had abandoned the city and returned to sharecropping in Mississippi. Memphis now had a population of 160,000, making it an even larger and more bewildering place than the city Wright's parents had encountered in 1911. Nonetheless Wright hoped he could realize the dream of urban success that had eluded his parents. Despite his general optimism, an awareness of his parents' crushed hopes must have colored Richard's mood as he retraced their steps, beginning his exploration of the city on Beale Street not far from where his father had been a night porter in a drugstore. He strolled up and down the street, soaking in his new surroundings while trying not to appear as naive and vulnerable as he felt.

He paused outside a large house with a sign advertising rooms for rent and was quickly greeted by a large, light-skinned African-American woman who was not fooled by his worldly airs. Recognizing him immediately as a disoriented migrant, she warmly ushered him inside the home and persuaded him to rent a room at a reduced rate. This unexpectedly friendly encounter with a Memphis resident thwarted Richard's expectations. His cool relationship with his family had not prepared him for this warm welcome or for the woman's offer to let him share meals with the family. He was further floored when the woman—who was impressed with Wright's solemn good manners and ambition—soon presented him with her daughter as a potential wife. Within a short time of leaving home, he had been offered admission into a new family and the opportunity to inherit a large house in the heart of Memphis's black community—a situation that would have been the envy of many of his school friends with their middle-class aspirations. He was simultaneously touched and repelled by the openness and kindness of his landlady and her daughter, but above all he was determined not to allow his plans to be waylaid. In contrast to his parents before him, Wright did not consider Memphis his ultimate destination. Instead he saw the city as a stopping point on a longer journey out of the South and on to Chicago, where he hoped he might finally escape from the racial prejudice and intellectual limitations of his childhood.

Although Wright experienced his trip to Memphis as a solitary journey, in the larger scheme of things he was hardly alone. His dreams of relocating to Chicago were stoked by the experiences of many others who had already traveled the same path, giving him reason to imagine his own escape. His flight from the South—for he self-consciously saw himself as nothing short of a refugee—was but a tiny tremor in an ongoing seismic population shift known as the Great Migration. Between 1916 and 1970 approximately seven million African Americans left the rural South in search of better economic opportunity and a less virulent racism.

Wright benefited from the pioneering efforts of the first significant wave of migrants who left the South while he was still a child, lured northward by jobs made suddenly available by the onset of World War I. These bold explorers sent word home about their experiences. Although none of them found a racial utopia in Chicago or any of the other

industrial cities that attracted black refugees, the consensus
was that there were opportunities in the North that were
unavailable to those who stayed in the South. Blacks in the
North could vote. They could send their children to better
schools. Above all, rural blacks from the South could hope
to earn a better living as industrial workers than they had as
sharecroppers. In general, circumstances in the North gave
African Americans an opportunity to circumvent some of
the more humiliating aspects of racial oppression; segregation was less rigid and the threat of racial violence more
muted there. Long before he left Mississippi, Wright had no
doubt been schooled in the limitations and possibilities of
the Great Migration, and he benefited from the shared collective experiences of the community when he made his
own fateful decision to flee.

Memphis served as something of a buffer zone between
the Deep South of Wright's childhood and the city of Chicago where he was to come of age intellectually. Although
the same racial mores held sway in both Jackson and Memphis, in the larger city Wright noted an "air of relative ur-
banity that took some of the sharpness off the attitude of
whites toward Negroes." In this environment he could at
long last find respite from some of the overwhelming anxiety he had felt while living in Mississippi. He quickly found
a job cleaning eyeglasses and running errands in an optical
factory, and devised a plan for frugal living that would enable him to save the needed funds to finance the second part
of his trip.

Although the less repressive atmosphere in Memphis
freed Wright from his preoccupation with lynch mobs, this
did not mean that his education in American racism had
ended. Indeed, as he describes it, the lives of his co-workers
were inextricably linked with those of the whites who employed them and worked alongside them. After all, their

scant livelihoods depended on their ability to maneuver on dangerous racial terrain—to appear genial and subservient without allowing themselves to be exploited. Wright's colleagues differed in their analysis of what constituted acceptable interracial interactions. Wright strove for privacy and a measured aloofness and was thus appalled by the behavior of Shorty, who operated the building's elevator. Wright could scarcely hide his disgust when he witnessed Shorty begging a white man for a quarter and then extracting the donation in exchange for giving the man permission to kick him, an opportunity the white man seized with relish. In *Black Boy*, Wright recalls witnessing this sordid exchange with horror. He could not, however, bring himself to argue with Shorty's crude, materialist explanation for his actions: "My ass is tough and quarters is scarce."

Wright soon found his attempts to comport himself with dignity rendered futile by the whites he worked alongside. One day the foreman took him aside and in conspiratorial tones warned him that Harrison, a young black man of about Wright's age, held a grudge against him and that Wright's physical safety was in danger. Richard cautiously approached Harrison and found that he too was being baited by whites who were trying to stir up animosity among the two young men for the sake of their own amusement. Due to the ethics of Jim Crow, neither Richard nor Harrison dared confront their tormentors directly and accuse them of lying. Instead they feigned ignorance and attempted to avoid each other, a strategy that worked for only a short time before the white men decided to stage a boxing match as a forum for the pair to settle their alleged grievances. Harrison agreed to participate in exchange for five dollars. Richard was far more reluctant, but he eventually gave in and was disgusted with himself when the fight turned more violent than the pair had intended as they misdirected their frustration with

Southern racism at each other. Humiliations like this one gnawed at Wright, leaving such a deep impression on his psyche that he continued to suffer from the wounds of his childhood and youth decades after leaving the segregated South.

Mercifully, his continued racial initiation was accompanied by a growing intellectual awakening that gave him the tools to better cope with the trauma of racism. Away from his grandmother's censorship, Wright began a period of intensive self-education. Although his frugality led him to subsist on a meager diet that included a nightly dinner of a can of pork and beans devoured secretly in his room, he was willing to spend some of his earnings on reading material, investing in secondhand books and magazines that he would resell when he was finished with them. For a time this serendipitous method of acquiring whatever literature was available was acceptable to him, but one day he read an editorial in the *Memphis Commercial Appeal* excoriating H. L. Mencken, editor of the *American Mercury.* Wright's curiosity was piqued: any enemy of the white Southern establishment was someone Wright wanted to know. He had to read Mencken, but how could he get his hands on one of his books? His thoughts immediately turned to the large Memphis public library, which blacks were not allowed to patronize. How could he skirt Southern segregation and satisfy his intellectual curiosity?

To supplement his income, Wright had often run errands for whites, taking trips to the dry cleaners, or to pick up lunch, or to the library. Although he did not have access to the library's card catalog, with a library card and a note from a white patron he had been allowed to check out specific books. Now he needed to find a sympathetic white person who would lend him a library card for his own use. In asking this favor, Wright was assuming a considerable risk. Not only was he trying to circumvent the laws of segregation, he was also exhibiting intellectual curiosity, a trait that contradicted every prevailing white stereotype about African Americans. Thinking carefully through his list of white acquaintances, and ruling most of them out for one reason or another, he finally settled upon an Irish Catholic man who was viewed dismissively by some white Southerners as a "Pope lover." Perhaps the man's outsider status would give him some empathy for Wright's predicament. He guessed correctly—the man agreed to let Wright use his library card. Eagerly, Wright wrote out these words, which have since become famous: "Dear Madam: Will you please let this nigger boy have some books by H. L. Mencken?" His true intentions cloaked behind that racial epithet, he could now begin in earnest his self-education.

The librarian handed him two books, *A Book of Prefaces* and *Prejudices.* For Wright, this encounter with Mencken was nothing short of life altering. It left him with the same breathless excitement he had felt as a child while listening to the whispered story of Bluebeard. Wright was struck by Mencken's bold writing style and his fearlessness. He realized that "this man was fighting, fighting with words. He was using words as a weapon, using them as one would a club." Wright began to hope that he too could learn to use words this way, to engage in a kind of warfare. He could combine his love of language and his curiosity about the world with his outrage about injustice. In writing about racism and eventually about his family, Wright could also indulge in a form of revenge by subjecting those who hurt him to the scrutiny of his readers.

After reading Mencken, he began devouring the books that Mencken alluded to, and in rapid succession introduced himself to writers ranging from Sherwood Anderson to Leo Tolstoy to T. S. Eliot. He was particularly touched by Theodore Dreiser, whose female characters gave him a broader framework in which to place his own mother's working-class experiences. Sinclair Lewis gave him the tools to better understand the interior life of his boss at the optical company. Instead of providing him with a form of escapism, his reading somehow connected him to others—even to those who misunderstood or despised him. With books as his companions, he suddenly felt less alone. But his integration into the world of ideas was also peculiarly accompanied by a "sense of guilt," for he feared that the whites around him were aware of his internal transformation and that he "had began to regard them differently." Thus his newfound knowledge was simultaneously liberating and a burden. Although reading great literature gave him a deeper sense of a shared human experience, Southern whites were no more likely to regard him with empathy than they had been before his awakening. He knew he could not remain in the South much longer.

Wright's mother and his brother Leon soon joined him in Memphis, and the three set up housekeeping with furniture paid for on an installment plan. Aunt Maggie, who had been abandoned by Professor Matthews, now joined them too. Her arrival prompted them finally to plan their escape. It was decided that Maggie and Richard would go north first, find jobs, and prepare a home for the family. After the plan had been hatched, Wright was left with the task of taking leave from his job. Although by now he had become more sophisticated in navigating the racial mores of the region, he knew that announcing his plans to go north would be met with suspicion from his co-workers who resented black migration. Swallowing his pride—an action he hoped he would have to perform less frequently in the future—he played the part of a helpless child who was being taken north against his will by his aunt and his mother. One of his co-workers articulated the fear of all Southern whites when he spat, "You'll change. Niggers change when they go north." As he boarded the train with his Aunt Maggie, Wright certainly hoped that this prediction would be correct.

Nothing in his experience had prepared Wright for his arrival in Chicago in 1927. With a population of nearly three million, the city made Memphis seem like a tiny hamlet. He was "depressed and dismayed" by the industrial landscape he encountered, the endless smokestacks that belched coal into the prairie sky and the smell of the stockyards, the livestock processing facilities that covered a square mile of Chicago's South Side. Although disoriented by the size of the city and by the industrial filth of the landscape, Wright could not help but feel relief as he noticed that his surroundings were not punctuated with the crude segregationist signs of his childhood, the signs mandating "Colored Entrance" or "Whites Only." He boarded an integrated streetcar, sat down beside a white man, and was thrilled to find that his presence was greeted with bland, urban indifference.

Despite the nonchalant coexistence between whites and blacks on the city streets, Wright soon discovered that Chicago was characterized by rigid residential segregation. At the time of Wright's arrival, more than 200,000 African Americans lived in the city, but most were clustered into what were then the Second and Third Wards of the South Side, bounded by Twenty-second Street on the north and Fifty-first Street on the south. The black neighborhood within this area was often dubbed the "Black Belt," but the residents of the area affectionately called it "Bronzeville," a nickname that more accurately described the skin color of most residents. A population explosion in Chicago had brought severe housing shortages, nowhere more so than in black neighborhoods. The restrictive housing covenants that barred blacks from renting or buying property in white majority districts were enforced by white residents who were willing to protect their neighborhoods from black incursions by violence if necessary.

In looking for housing, African Americans had few places to turn and were often forced to pay exorbitant rents to live in dilapidated tenements. To meet the demand for housing, developers made enormous profits by carving existing apartments into small, one room units known as "kitchenettes." Entire families would often reside in these single rooms, and the resulting overcrowding placed a tremendous strain on shared bathroom facilities, leading to poor sanitary conditions. Landlords had no incentive to maintain decaying buildings as units would be rented regardless of their condition. On the other hand, because of the housing shortage the city could not easy demolish buildings that should have been condemned. One look at the South Side slums was enough to convince Wright that white Chicagoans were no more immune from racism than white Mississippians. Otherwise the city leaders would not have allowed black residents to live in such dehumanizing conditions.

No doubt Wright was disheartened when his journey from Memphis came to its immediate conclusion at his Aunt Cleo's ramshackle kitchenette. Aunt Maggie chose to stay with friends elsewhere in the city while Wright rented a room of his own from Aunt Cleo's landlady and set about trying to find his way in this strange new place. In his search for employment, Wright ruled out industrial jobs. Years of malnutrition had made him weak and unfit for strenuous physical work. But he quickly found a job running errands for the owners of a Jewish delicatessen and later as a dishwasher at a bustling café.

His first employment experiences in the North were tainted by his years of training about survival in the South, and he responded to his white employers and co-workers accordingly. He lied to the owner of the delicatessen when he needed a day off to prepare for a job examination at the post office—a relatively high-paying job open to African Americans. His Southern employers had consistently tried to thwart his ambitions, and he could not believe that his new boss could be more charitable. But his lie led to hurt feelings on both sides, and Wright left his job in shame, vowing in the future not to let his Southern past poison his current relationships. In his next job as a dishwasher he was amazed to notice how casually his white female co-workers treated him, unthinkingly squeezing against him in the confines of a small kitchen, a shocking contrast to Southern white women who avoided proximity to black men at all costs.

Richard saved as much money as he could from working at the café, and he and Maggie combined their resources, rented a two-room apartment, and invited Leon and Ella to join them. Eventually Granny Wilson moved to Chicago too. For the next nine years of his life, Wright lived in a series of tiny apartments with his family members. His time in Memphis had made him accustomed to a measure of independence, and living in close quarters with them again proved to be a difficult adjustment. Although he worked diligently to support his fragile mother, aging grandmother, and brother who also suffered from health problems, his efforts on their behalf were not enough to bridge the divide that had sprung up between them during Wright's childhood. The women in Wright's family were still bewildered at his interest in exploring the life of the mind, and even his beloved Aunt Maggie accused him of running up the electric bill with his incessant reading.

Wright was overjoyed when, after scoring in the ninety-fourth percentile on a competitive examination, in June 1928 he was offered a temporary job sorting mail at the post office. He would make almost twice the pay he had made at the café, and his regular eight-hour workdays would leave him with more free time to devote to reading and writing. By now he was spending the bulk of his free time doing writing exercises. Sitting in his dingy room, he would construct florid sentences about melting butter or sleeping children, out of a compulsion to manipulate the language. His vociferous appetite for books had helped him improve his vocabulary. From reading other writers, he had tutored himself on the techniques of the craft.

After acquiring these fundamental skills, he determined to use his writing to describe the realities of everyday African-American life. To do this, he believed, he needed a framework broader than his own subjective experience, and he began reading widely in sociology and psychology in order to better understand his environment and indeed his experiences. His eternal feeling of being something of an outsider in the black community made it easy for him to adopt the posture of the social scientist and to live as a perpetual participant-observer, making detached mental notes on his daily life that he would later analyze through his writing.

His post office job was in many ways ideal. Not only were the pay high and the hours conducive to his desire to spend time writing, but his co-workers were an intellectually stimulating group. The Chicago post office was playfully dubbed "the university" because of the many employees who worked there while attending college. For Wright, the daily opportunity to dialogue with this more educated crowd served as a substitute for a college experience, and he learned all he could. For the first time in his life he was surrounded by people who shared his interest in the written word, and he enjoyed having long conversations about literature while sorting the mail. He faced a major obstacle, however, if he wished to see the temporary job become permanent. He would have to pass a physical examination at the end of the summer, and the minimum weight requirement for a regular post office employee was 125 pounds. After years of being malnourished, Wright weighed a mere 110, and he feared he would be unable to gain the necessary weight despite stuffing himself with high-protein foods for weeks. He was right.

After failing the examination, Wright returned to his job at the café and began gorging himself, determined to gain enough weight to regain his former position. Triumphantly, in the spring of 1929 he met his weight goal and was offered the job of a temporary clerk. He had every reason to believe that his appointment would become permanent. His good wages enabled him to rent a four-bedroom apartment for his family at 4831 Vincennes Avenue, offering them a respite from the crowded conditions of slum life. But the improvement in their circumstances was short-lived. After the stock market crashed in 1929, the post office failed to renew his contract, and the Wright family's brief period of relative affluence ended.

It was during this financially bleak time that Wright published his first story written as an adult. To this point he had thrown away most of his private writing experiments, judging them crude and immature. While working at the post office, however, he finally summoned the courage to submit a short story to *Abbott's Monthly*. He was thrilled when he learned that "Superstition" by Richard Nathaniel Wright was to appear in the magazine's April 1931 issue. *Abbott's* had been created by distinguished editor Robert Abbott, founder of the *Chicago Defender*, the leading black newspaper in Chicago. It was an impressive venture that printed 100,000 copies each issue, giving Wright a wide audience for his work. The story, as the title indicates, was concerned with the supernatural. The tale is about a group of middle-class African-American businessmen who sit around a table after dinner telling fantastic stories. One of the men recounts the hardships of a family that experiences the death of a member each year during a family reunion. The tone is reminiscent of Edgar Allan Poe and bears little resemblance to the naturalistic fiction that was to make Wright famous. Instead it represents an early attempt both to find an authorial voice and to cater to the tastes of his imagined middle-brow audience through a suspenseful, atmospheric tale.

Wright was distressed when *Abbott's Monthly* succumbed to the economic crisis and folded without ever paying him for his story. His failure to receive his pay was much more than a matter of principle to him: he had been reduced to working odd jobs, often finding himself without work. Among other things, he was paid to collect votes for "Big Bill" Thompson, the Republican mayor, a task he did for the money rather than out of political conviction. In desperation, he later accepted the even more distasteful job of selling burial insurance on a commission basis to poor blacks. His own financial neediness compelled him do things he found morally repugnant, including stealthily swapping out insurance policies that promised high premiums with new documents that offered less generous terms. Like many other black insurance salesman, he often yielded to the temptation of accepting sex in lieu of the ten-cent weekly premium from some of his neediest female clients. He was almost relieved when that job too ended and he was left to find less morally dubious ways to earn a living.

During the Great Depression Wright experienced firsthand the reality of being African American. In the 1930s black unemployment reached 50 percent as blacks found that during economic downturns they were typically the "last hired and first fired." For a time too Wright found himself out of work, and he was forced to seek public relief. After years of working hard and never seeking charity in spite of material deprivation, asking city officials for food for his family was a humiliating experience, but it was also a revelatory one. He saw that he was hardly alone in his desperation, and he felt spiritually and politically connected to his fellow sufferers, people he was beginning to see as victims of the system of capitalism that made some people rich at the expense of others. He realized that despite his perpetual feeling of intellectual isolation, in purely material terms his circumstances were far from unique. As he sat in a crowded room waiting for his turn to, as he termed it, "beg bread," his normal cynicism temporarily abated and he began to meditate on the possibilities of collective action should the poor and the dispossessed find a unified way to act.

Wright's anxiety about feeding himself and his family may have been overpowering, but he did not allow this most fundamental concern to interfere with his growing obsession with writing. His desire to write complemented rather than detracted from his rising political consciousness, for he began to believe that good writing had the power to help effect social change. Although he had mixed feelings about the quality of the story he had published in *Abbott's Monthly*, it did affirm his hope that he could find an audience for his work. In addition to spending most of his free time writing, Wright also began to seek out the company of like-minded people with whom he could discuss his work. In the autumn of 1933 he began spending the occasional evening with a group of white friends he had met at the post office. They would gather in Abraham Aaron's room and talk late into the night over salami sandwiches and beer. During these drawn-out conversations that touched on political as well as literary matters, Wright discovered that many of these men had either joined or were sympathetic to the Communist party.

Although Wright's experiences on welfare had instilled in him feelings of class solidarity, his identification with other members of the poor and working classes had not yet included the Communists who sought to speak for this group. Wright was more interested in art than in politics, and to the extent that he was politically inclined, he felt more innate sympathy for the followers of the black nationalist Marcus Garvey than for members of the Communist party. He was profoundly touched by the "totally racialistic outlook" of the Garveyites, which "endowed them with a dignity [he] had never seen before in Negroes." Although Wright regarded their dream of "returning" to an Africa they had never known as nothing more than a pipe dream, he could identify with their profound disillusionment with life in the United States. In contrast, he was far less impressed with the black Communists he encountered.

The Great Depression provided fertile climate for the recruiting efforts of both Communists and socialists, whose critique of capitalism seemed more salient than ever in light of massive unemployment, home evictions, and food shortages. The message of the Communist party had a particular resonance for some African Americans because the party was explicitly anti-racist in its policies. Its defense of black rights was far from merely rhetorical. The Communist-backed International Labor Defense fund proved willing to take on the cases of African Americans who had been unfairly treated by the U.S. legal system, including, most famously, the Scottsboro Boys, nine young black men who had been wrongly accused of rape in Alabama in 1931. The Communists also went so far as to expel party members who were found guilty of racist behavior.

In an era when the mainstream political parties were unwilling to take strong affirmative stances on pressing civil rights issues, including anti-lynching legislation and the disfranchisement of Southern blacks, the Communists' un-compromising assault on racism was understandably appeal-ing to many. Nowhere were the Communists more success-ful in their efforts to recruit black members than in Chicago. In 1930 the 233,903 African Americans living in Chicago comprised 6.9 percent of the city's population, but their rep-resentation among the ranks of the Communist party was much higher. Four hundred twelve black Communists made up 24.3 percent of the membership of the Chicago branch.

Ardent Communists were a vocal presence on the South Side. Wright was accustomed to hearing them speak on street corners, and he was initially unimpressed with what he saw and heard. Some of the Communist recruits had, in Wright's view, transformed themselves into caricatures rather than into believable political agents. He was scorn-ful of the fact that they wore caps like the one Lenin wore and modified their speech to sound like white Communists, many of them recent immigrants. He was disgusted to over-hear native English speakers speak of the "parrrtee," em-phasizing the second syllable in an attempt to sound like their white comrades who spoke the language with a heavy accent. He was even more appalled at the anti-intellectual-ism of some of the stump speakers: "They denounced books they had never read, people they had never known, ideas they could never understand, and doctrines whose names they could not pronounce."

These negative impressions of Communists caused Wright to feel some unease when his friend Aaron revealed that he had joined the party. But he also felt a deep sense of kinship to Aaron because he, like Wright, desperately wanted to become a writer. Thus Wright was faced with a dilemma when his friend invited him to attend a meeting of the Chicago John Reed Club. Reed had been an American journalist who had gone to Russia to see for himself the Bolshevik Revolution, and had written *Ten Days That Shook the World,* a sympathetic account that became widely read. He went on to become one of the founding members of the Communist Party of the United States of America (CPUSA). After his sudden death from typhus in 1920, he was buried as a hero in the Kremlin. By this time the club of proletarian artists and writers named in his honor counted more than thirty chapters in cities throughout the United States.

Although the club's ties to the CPUSA were well known, party membership was not a prerequisite for joining, a fact that emboldened Wright to visit. The Chicago branch met on Michigan Avenue just south of the Loop and claimed about a hundred, mostly white members who were invited to meetings each Tuesday night and to a lecture series on Saturday nights. When Wright climbed a narrow stairway to the group's office and opened the door, he found a cluttered office space brimming with overflowing ashtrays and strewn papers. The walls were painted with murals depicting strong and triumphant members of the proletariat. He received a warm welcome; with no questions asked he was invited to join a meeting of the club's literary magazine, *Left Front,* which was then in progress. He left that night feeling impressed with the courteous reception he had received by the white members of the club and carrying a number of back issues of the left-leaning magazine *New Masses.*

He did not realize it then, but he later recalled that at this first encounter with the John Reed Club "I was meeting men and women whom I would know for decades to come, who were to form the first sustained relationships of my life." He went home to his shabby apartment and began reading the literature he had been given. He was enthralled by what he saw as "an organized search for truth of the lives of the oppressed and isolated," an undertaking that seemed akin to what he hoped to accomplish with his own writing.

The contributors to these magazines exhibited the same quality he had admired in H. L. Mencken: they used words as weapons. He could not help but feel inspired by the revolutionary fervor exhibited in those pages, by the idea that it might be possible to build a more just and equitable world. He was not sure, however, that the writers in *Left Front* and *New Masses* had found the proper language to describe accurately the experiences of ordinary people, particularly black people. Inspired, he began his own attempts to use literature to capture the voices of the working class.

Feverishly, Wright now began writing poetry. Although he was ultimately to become famous as a writer of prose, in this early period he became known for his proletarian poetry. While faithfully attending club meetings, he would bring along a verse or two for his fellow members to critique. In February 1934, *Left Front* published two of his poems. Soon after, Jack Conroy accepted two more for publication in his recently founded journal the *Anvil*. The very best of these early poems, "I Have Seen Black Hands" was printed in *New Masses*. The poem attempts to evoke the diversity, beauty, and tragedy of the black experience as Wright describes black hands reaching for objects ranging from peppermint sticks and the guns of the military to spinning tops and industrial machinery. The final, triumphant stanza imagines a bright future for a unified, interracial working class:

> I am black and I have seen black hands
> Raised in fists of revolt, side by side with the white fists of white workers,
> And some day—and it is only this which sustains me—
> Some day there shall be millions and millions of them,
> On some red day in a burst of fists on the new horizon!

Not long after his first visit to the John Reed Club, his work was being eagerly published by some of the left's most important literary journals, and he had made a series of lasting friendships with talented writers. He had also impressed Jack Conroy, one of the most important left-wing novelists of the period. Nelson Algren, yet to do his most significant work, also became a close friend. At this time he also formed relationships with two white women who were to become important readers of some of his early attempts at fiction. He met Joyce Gourfain at the club and almost certainly had an affair with her. She introduced Wright to the work of Henry James and proved to be a perceptive, if at times impatient, reader for successive drafts of what was to become one of Wright's best-known short stories, "Down by the Riverside," inspired by the Mississippi River flood of 1927. In this powerful story, the symbolically named protagonist "Mann" battles both nature and racism as he futilely attempts to save the life of his sick and pregnant wife. Wright's platonic friendship with Jane Newton, wife of the prominent South Side black Communist Herbert Newton, also proved to be of remarkable importance in his development as a writer of fiction. Jane and Richard had long, detailed conversations about the intricacies of the plots of his short stories and later about what was to become his best-selling novel, *Native Son*.

After years of feeling misunderstood by his family and by other members of his community, Wright was exhilarated by the company of like-minded people who were enthusiastic about his prospects as a writer. As he threw himself into the life of the John Reed Club, he soon discovered tensions between those who belonged to the CPUSA and those who were merely sympathetic to its aims. When the club decided to elect a new executive secretary, Wright was shocked to find himself—a member for only a few months—nominated for the position and even more surprised when he was elected. He resigned from the post immediately, arguing that as a newcomer he was not yet ready to lead; but the other members refused to let him step down.

Later he learned that his election was part of the crude political infighting between the club's different factions. The non-Communist members sought to weaken the Communist influence by electing a leader who was not a member of the party. They correctly gambled that party members would be reluctant to vote against a black candidate lest they be charged with racial chauvinism. Regardless of the circumstances surrounding his election, Wright took his job seriously and became deeply invested in the success of the organization. When a party member told Wright that he would have to officially join the party or resign from his position, he felt as though he had little choice. The club now meant too much to him. He informed the party that his primary interest as a party member would be in nurturing the development of writers and artists, and he signed up.

If this decision had not been forced on him, Wright might have remained a sympathetic outsider. But he generally agreed with the party's aims. He had no great affection for the U.S. government, which allowed institutionalized racism to thrive. He welcomed the idea of a revolution and of a new society run by the working class. His greater contact with party members had forced him to complicate his earlier evaluations of the Communists he had scornfully scrutinized on the street corners of the South Side. He was inspired by certain elements of their message and dared believe in the possibility of interracial cooperation, even though his years in the Jim Crow South had shown him little evidence that such a thing could be possible. A decade after joining the party, he looked back at his period of indoctrination and recalled, "My attention was caught by the similarity of the experiences of workers in other lands, by the possibility of uniting scattered but kindred peoples into a whole."

Wright's election as secretary did not smooth over political differences between the members of the club. One of the major issues of disagreement was the role of writers and artists in the revolutionary struggle. Wright firmly believed that the artist's primary task was to perfect his or her technique. Others believed that artists should spend part of each day at work on their crafts but that the rest of their time should be spent doing other kinds of work for the CPUSA. This theory appeared reasonable but was scarcely a feasible plan of action for writers like Wright, who were employed full time trying to earn a living while writing on the side. Wright argued that there were not enough hours in the day to do everything, and that the job of a revolutionary artist— above all—was to create art that reflected the experience of the working class.

Although he expressed his opinion forcefully, his arguments fell on deaf ears. Growing concern that publishing was distracting the members of the John Reed Club from their other party obligations was coupled with mounting financial pressures, and the *Left Front* was voted out of existence. Wright got the sense that this decision was made by higher-ups in the party rather than an outgrowth of the will of club members. Disgusted, he grumbled that the club too should be dissolved if the journal were discontinued.

This rash suggestion came true when the Communist party decided to abandon the John Reed Clubs altogether. The decision was made as part of a major shift in party policy in 1935 known as the Popular Front. Largely in response to the rise of Nazism in Germany, American Communists were ordered by Moscow to set aside partisan differences and cooperate with members outside the party who shared some of its goals, particularly opposition to German fascism. The party decided that the John Reed Clubs were no longer suitable to this new political environment, that there was a need for more inclusive organizations of writers and artists. This decision was a crushing blow to Wright, for the club had become the center of his life—socially, politically, and artistically.

In despair, Wright went to New York in April 1935 to attend the American Writers Congress, which had been organized by the Communist party as an opportunity for left-leaning writers to gather to discuss not only their craft but also their shared political interests. By now he was having trouble maintaining his earlier optimism about his potential to thrive as an artist while being a member of the Communist party. He was further disillusioned, upon his arrival in New York, to discover that the organizers of the conference had neglected to take his race into account when arranging overnight accommodations for delegates. When he appeared at the meeting, flustered organizers realized that they had not yet found anyone willing to accommodate a black comrade overnight. Finally, someone offered Wright a cot in her kitchen.

Angry that his white comrades were not as free from racism as their rhetorical posturing would indicate, the next day Wright found his own way to Harlem. There he was turned away from a hotel situated in the heart of the black community that accepted only white guests. His difficulties in finding a place to sleep further soured his mood during the proceedings of the Congress. He spoke up forcefully but futilely against the decision to dissolve the John Reed Clubs and in so doing made himself known as someone who would not meekly submit to party rulings.

The CPUSA replaced the clubs with the League of American Writers, which was to be a broad coalition of writers on the political left. Although Wright was appointed a member of the group, he was distressed at this turn of events. He was not prepared to sever his ties to the party as many of his social relationships and most of his publishing connections flowed from it. But his tenuous belief that the party might help usher in a golden era of interracial harmony and the ascendancy of the working classes was shattered. Although he admired many Communist ideas and the moral seriousness of the party members he knew, he could see that the human beings charged with carrying out these ideas were deeply flawed.

Even as Wright grappled with the political questions raised by his involvement with the CPUSA, he still had to contend with the problem of feeding himself and his family during the lean years of the Great Depression. He worked at a variety of jobs—hospital orderly, street sweeper, ditchdigger, and supervisor at the South Side Boys' Club. He proved to be an adaptable and hard worker, and the experiences he gained during this tumultuous period of his life gave him important insights that found their way into his fiction. His experiences at the South Side Boys' Club in particular tutored him on the background, speech patterns, and aspirations of many young black men who came of age in Chicago. He later used these details to create his best-known protagonist, Bigger Thomas, a young man who comes of age on the South Side and whose experiences in that hostile environment transform him into someone capable of murder.

As enriching as this variety of work experiences was, Wright was thrilled when in 1935 he was offered a position in the Illinois Federal Writers' Project, an employment program for writers that was part of Franklin D. Roosevelt's New Deal. In a relatively short period of time he went from being a street sweeper to a professional writer on the payroll of the federal government. As an FWP employee, Wright did some publicity for the Federal Negro Theater. Upon his arrival at this project in 1936, he was appalled by the choice of plays the company was staging, which he thought promoted

racial stereotypes and failed to engage the realities of con-
temporary black life. He responded to the situation with
his usual brash self-confidence, convinced that his aesthetic
and political judgment was superior to that of the troupe of
actors who made up the theater group. He sprang into action
and convinced the project to hire Charles DeSheim, a talented Jewish director, to stage a realistic play about life on
a Southern chain gang written by Paul Green. To Wright's
dismay, the actors rebelled against this decision and quickly
began mobilizing to get DeSheim removed from the project.
They preferred uplifting, lighthearted dramas and resented
Wright, characterizing him as a race traitor because of his
strong support for the white director. Both DeSheim and
Wright, fearing for their personal safety, were quickly trans-
ferred off the project. Once again Wright was faced with the
dilemma of his uneasy relationship with the black community. Although he wanted to convey the reality of the black
experience to a broader public, other African Americans
were skeptical of his vision.

Not only had Wright inspired the ire of black actors on
the theater project, he seemed continually to infuriate his
fellow Communists as well. After the John Reed Clubs were
dissolved, Wright had less contact with party activities. His
very standoffishness violated the party ethos. A decision to
join the CPUSA was considered to be synonymous with a total
commitment, including submission to party discipline. At
the very least, this called for attendance at lengthy meetings
several nights each week. Simultaneously trying to work
full time, fulfill party obligations, and establish oneself as a
writer was, as Wright discovered, all but impossible. His rare
appearances at unit meetings, coupled with his well-known
disdain for the decision to dissolve the John Reed Clubs,
made him suddenly suspect in party circles. Word reached
Wright that he had been branded as, among other things, a

"bastard intellectual." His assertiveness, his desire to set his own schedule and voice his own opinions, made him anathema to a party apparatus that demanded strict obedience.

One day when he was in bed recovering from a virus, a party member showed up with an invitation that Wright, despite his growing disillusionment, felt he could not refuse: Harry Haywood wanted to see him. Haywood had initially become involved in the CPUSA through the African Blood Brotherhood, a black nationalist organization that subscribed to Marxist principles. By the time Wright met him he was a member of the Central Committee of the party and had been instrumental in party policy related to the so-called Negro Question in the United States. Haywood helped develop the idea that black people living in black majority areas of the South had the right to self-determination and should be allowed to form a separate nation. Although his accomplishments would have been well known to Wright, when Wright met him face to face he was struck by Haywood's "greasy, sweaty" looks and his awkward manner of speaking in "short, jerky" sentences.

Haywood had summoned Wright to test the limits of his loyalty by asking him to organize a committee to study the "high cost of living." Once again Wright was confronted with the dilemma that tainted his final days at the John Reed Club—the problem of finding time to write while appeasing the leadership of the party. Wright passionately expressed his reluctance to take on the assignment, explaining once again that the first responsibility of a revolutionary writer was to write well and to write truly, and this required constant effort. He was not inclined to tabulate the price of groceries while his unfinished manuscripts lay untouched in his shabby bedroom. He left the meeting without making a formal commitment. His meeting with Haywood may have reminded him of his childhood confrontations with Granny.

By temperament, Wright resented being told what to do and how to live, and he was nearly as repelled by Haywood's rigid political zealotry as he had been by his family's religious devotion.

In Wright's 1944 essay, "I Tried to Be a Communist," he recalled that his meeting with Haywood made him realize that "I wanted to be a Communist, but my kind of Communist. I wanted to shape people's feeling, awaken their hearts." The CPUSA wanted him to run long meetings where he would offer strategies to deal with the cost of housing and utilities—issues that someone in Wright's predicament was sure to care about. Wright, however, needed to create fictional worlds that he could use to explore the problems of this real one. He had fled the South because there he had been stifled intellectually; he could not allow his creative energies to be dampened by the designs that Haywood and others had for him.

Buoyed by a new clarity after his meeting with Haywood, and by the realization that he could not now or ever sacrifice his intellectual or artistic independence, he publicly announced his desire to be removed by party rolls. This separation, he claimed, was not ideological but practical. He did not wish to be given party orders, which his temperament made it impossible for him to obey.

This initial break with the party did not prove to be a final separation. Nonetheless Wright paid a high price for his assertion of intellectual independence. His assignment for the Federal Writers' Project was to help produce a guidebook for the State of Illinois as part of the American Guide series. Many of his fellow writers on the project were party members who now shunned him as a traitor. He bitterly recalled that other former comrades violently shoved him when he spontaneously attempted to march beside them in a May Day parade. Still, he remained undaunted. In fighting for his freedom he had made the only decision he felt he could. He fought his Communist comrades with the same tenacity that he had argued against Granny's mandates as a child.

For the time being Wright would continue his quest for community elsewhere. True to his inclination, he chose to concentrate on his craft rather than on politics, and he found support in his efforts from a group of talented and ambitious African-American writers. Beginning in April 1936, at Wright's urging, about twenty black writers gathered every other Sunday to discuss their work. Members of this South Side Writers' Group talked about the particular challenges faced by their generation of black writers who were artistically coming of age just as the Harlem Renaissance was drawing to a close. Members of the group included Arna Bontemps, who had been an important figure during the Harlem Renaissance, and Margaret Walker, who was in the earliest stages of transforming herself into one of the most important African-American writers of her generation. Surrounded by this group of serious and talented writers, Wright felt confident of the choice he had made. Above all, he must write. Weary after his battles with the Communists, he began to suspect that he had exhausted his opportunities in Chicago. In 1937 he decided that the logical next step on his journey would be to relocate to New York, the literary capital of the United States.

CHAPTER THREE

Breakthrough

ᴪ During his years in Chicago, many editors sympathetic to the Communist party found Wright's writing irresistible. Not only were flashes of startling insight and talent evident even in his earliest and clumsiest attempts, but as a black proletariat writer he was the incarnation of two key party values—anti-racism and the promotion of working-class art. To this point, however, Wright had been less successful in finding mainstream publishing venues for his writing. This was despite the fact that he wrote steadily and prolifically throughout the decade that he lived in Chicago.

By 1935 he had completed a draft of a novel he called "Cesspool," which he submitted to publishers unsuccessfully over the course of two years. Drawing inspiration from James Joyce's *Ulysses*, the novel chronicles one day in the life of Jake Jackson, a disgruntled husband and Chicago post office employee. The book is not as explicitly polemical as Wright's later prose, but he hints at a broader analysis by setting the events of the novel on Lincoln's birthday. By juxtaposing Jake's actions with information about the Great Emancipator's life, presented as the text from a radio broadcast, it is clear that Wright views his fictional creation as still enslaved—to his own appetites for violence, women, and booze; to an unsatisfying job; and to a bleak urban environment. Wright's descriptions of lower-class black life on Chicago's South Side are well drawn, but publishers rejected the novel nonetheless, citing reasons ranging from a thin plot to an unlikable, brutish protagonist. Discouraged, Wright abandoned hope of finding a publisher for the manuscript, which ultimately appeared posthumously in 1963 as *Lawd Today!*

When Wright decided to move to New York to pursue his writing career, he was making a giant leap of faith. His most substantial creative work to date had been rejected by the publishing world, but his belief in his own talent propelled him forward. Any uncertainty he might have felt about his future success as a writer was compounded by the fact that just as he was prepared to leave, he was finally offered the long-coveted permanent position in the post office. The promised salary of $2,100 a year would have enabled him to support both himself and his family in comfort even in the midst of the depression. But the same restlessness and ambition that had pushed him out of Mississippi as a malnourished and poorly educated teenager guided him again as he left the familiar comfort of the world he had created for himself in Chicago. With a mere forty dollars in his pocket and no job awaiting him, in June 1937 he set out for New York.

Wright applied for a transfer to the New York office of the Federal Writers' Project, but while he waited to learn the fate of his application he still needed work. He quickly found himself thrust back into Communist circles. Despite his conflicts with party officials in Chicago, the organization was reluctant to lose the talented writer. The New York party offered him the position of Harlem editor for the party newspaper, the *Daily Worker.* Although this was not his dream assignment, Wright found it more compelling than organizing against the high cost of living, and he was grateful for the paycheck. He went on to write more than two

hundred articles for the *Worker*, most of them published
without a byline. The vast majority were short, perfunctory
pieces reporting on events of interest to Harlem residents,
including details about famous visitors to the neighborhood,
local protests against the Italian invasion of Ethiopia, and
demonstrations against racial violence in the South. But he
also wrote a few longer pieces where he dramatically captured the living conditions of Harlem's poor and described
important cultural events. This kind of reporting was much
more to Wright's liking, allowing him to suffuse the dry
techniques of journalism with the language of literature in
documenting the textures of daily life.

During the six months he worked for the newspaper, he
became intimately acquainted with this storied African-
American neighborhood. From his furnished hotel room,
Wright could see that the area suffered from many of the
same symptoms of racial exclusion and poverty as the South
Side of Chicago. Harlem in the 1930s was more than twice
as densely populated as other New York neighborhoods,
and because blacks faced housing discrimination elsewhere,
landlords were able to charge exorbitant rents to black tenants for even dilapidated dwellings. High unemployment,
lack of educational opportunity, exorbitant prices for food
and other basic necessities, and police brutality were char-
acteristics of life in Harlem. His time there made a lasting
impression on him. Later, after he became well known as a
writer, Wright used his influence to help raise money for the
Lafargue Clinic, founded by his friend Frederic Wertham to
provide psychiatric services for Harlem's troubled youth. He
also explored the social problems of the area fictively in *The
Jackal*, an unpublished novel about juvenile delinquency.

Despite Harlem's social problems, the area retained an
important place in the African-American imagination. Black
settlement in the neighborhood had begun around the turn

of the twentieth century after a crash in real estate prices led to a scarcity of white tenants, causing Harlem landlords to reluctantly rent apartments to African Americans desperate for a reprieve from the slum conditions and racial tensions that existed in many lower Manhattan neighborhoods. Black migration into the neighborhood squeezed out the white residents, who by 1930 were all but gone, leaving behind a thriving black community that became the symbolic capital of black America. The poet Langston Hughes famously referred to the 1920s, the decade when it was clear that the scales had been tipped and that Harlem had become an African-American mecca, as the decade when the "Negro was in vogue."

Indeed the decade had witnessed an outpouring of black political energy and artistic expression centered in upper Manhattan. The National Association for the Advancement of Colored People and Marcus Garvey's Universal Negro Improvement Association were both headquartered there. Members of the NAACP mobilized visibly in protest against racism in its various manifestations. Garvey's followers sought to empower the black community, combating racism by building black businesses and cultivating race pride. Black writers like Countee Cullen, Claude McKay, and Jessie Fauset found larger audiences than ever before for their creative work, as did visual artists like Aaron Douglas and Augusta Savage. The sounds of jazz and the blues could be heard coming from well-established as well as makeshift nightclubs throughout the neighborhood, and many white New Yorkers began venturing into the area, some to flirt with the idea of integration, others to imbibe some of the artistic energy from the relative safety of racially segregated hotspots like the Cotton Club.

Wright had, of course, missed out on the glory days of Harlem in the twenties. When Langston Hughes arrived in New York to enroll in Columbia University in 1921, Wright was still a child rebelling against his twin torments of Southern racism and his grandmother's strict religious codes. By the time he got to New York, the Harlem Renaissance had all but faded, crushed by the weight of the depression. The mood of the era, however, had not fully dissipated. Harlem remained a hotbed of political activism, and the embers of the once white-hot artistic movement continued to glow. Zora Neale Hurston, one of the premier writers of the Harlem Renaissance, published her best-known novel, *Their Eyes Were Watching God*, the year Wright arrived in Harlem.

Although Harlem captured Wright's imagination during his years in New York, he spent little time actually living there, preferring more peaceful surroundings in Brooklyn or in Greenwich Village. After writing for the *Daily Worker* for six months he began, once again, to chafe at the restrictions of party membership. Reporting only on items of interest in party circles and holding his analysis within the strict confines of party ideology limited his creativity. Soon he began to resent the drudgery of working for the newspaper, longing instead for complete artistic freedom to write about subjects *he* found compelling. He was relieved to learn, in December 1937, that the Federal Writers' Project had approved his transfer to the New York office. Ironically, though, his assignment there was to work on the Harlem sections of a New York guidebook.

Coming of age artistically as he did at the tail end of Harlem's artistic explosion, Wright was obliged to grapple with the meaning of this Renaissance and to view his own work in relation to what had come before him. He had already developed relationships with some Renaissance luminaries, including Langston Hughes and Arna Bontemps, individuals who continued to create long after the explosive 1920s.

After moving to New York, Wright began collaborating with Dorothy West, one of the youngest writers associated with the Renaissance. In 1926 her short story "The Typewriter" had earned her second place in a writing contest sponsored by *Opportunity* magazine, earning the precocious nineteen-year-old the nickname "the Kid." In 1934, in an attempt to revive the fading literary movement, West created a literary journal called *Challenge,* which ran for six issues and published many of the most notable black writers of the era. In 1937 she decided to reinvent the journal in a more self-consciously political direction. She asked Richard Wright and Marian Minus, another member of Wright's South Side Writers' Group, to join her in editing what was to be called *New Challenge.*

Editorial differences were clear from the outset. West felt affronted by the aggressive role Wright took in shaping the content of the journal and in advertising it in the Communist press. When the one and only issue of the magazine appeared, Wright had been demoted to associate editor on the cover, but his vision prevailed in the pages of the journal. It contained pieces written by a number of his friends, including Margaret Walker and Frank Marshall Davis from Chicago and Ralph Ellison, a new acquaintance.

Seven years Wright's junior, Ellison had fled to New York from Tuskegee University in 1936, a year shy of graduating. He had been plagued with money problems throughout his college years and had grown weary of finding ways to gather the necessary funds to stay in school. Although he had met kindred spirits at Tuskegee, as a whole he found the students there intellectually dull, and he had personality conflicts with many of the institution's leaders. Craving a more cosmopolitan setting, Ellison traveled north to pursue his dual interests of classical music performance and sculpture. Like many other African-American intellectuals, he was drawn to the egalitarianism of the Communist party and began reading left-wing publications. There he discovered Wright's poetry and was impressed. Ellison was interested in the style of modern literature as practiced by T. S. Eliot and Ezra Pound, and he saw traces of their influence in Wright's work.

Langston Hughes, a tireless advocate of younger aspiring black artists and writers, was acquainted with both men and provided an introduction. Soon Ellison was spending a great deal of time hanging around the offices of the *Daily Worker*, watching Wright in action. Wright liked Ellison's intellect, and he encouraged him to try his hand at writing, something the variously talented younger man had never considered. At Wright's urging, Ellison wrote a review of Waters Turpin's novel *These Low Grounds*, which appeared in *New Challenge*. The serendipitous series of events that led to Ellison's first publication propelled him to abandon his aspirations as a visual artist and a professional musician. Under Wright's tutelage he began to concentrate on his writing. His change in direction was to bear fruit in 1953 when his ambitious novel *Invisible Man* received the National Book Award. For almost a decade, Ellison was both Wright's protégé and his closest friend.

Wright's own contribution to *New Challenge*, "Blueprint for Negro Writing," articulated his artistic philosophy along with a searing critique of the Harlem Renaissance. He labeled his predecessors "decorous ambassadors who went a-begging to white America." Black writers, he argued, were self-indulgent in producing art for its own sake and misguided in believing that art could be effective in persuading white America to grant African Americans true equality. Black art should be made for the common people and used to help shape their consciousness, a consciousness inspired by Marxism, he declared. In writing this essay, Wright an-

Ralph Ellison in 1950. A future National Book Award winner, Ellison was Wright's protégé and closest friend while he lived in New York. *(Library of Congress)*

nounced his break with the past and defended his belief in social realism as a powerful polemical tool. He also alienated Dorothy West, who found Wright's tone too strident and who ceased publishing *New Challenge* after a single issue.

Fortunately for Wright, during the bleak depression years many American critics and readers were receptive to works created in the style of social realism he favored. Seizing upon the somber atmosphere of the moment, writers and visual artists began producing art that sought to capture realistic snapshots of American life, particularly working-class life. Writers like Nelson Algren, photographers such as Walker

Evans, and painters including Isaac Soyer used their craft to document and explore a variety of social ills. Wright wanted to use the vehicle of social realism to describe the impact of racism on its victims and to indict American society for tolerating the systemic injustices that plagued black people.

Despite how the mood of the times seemed to fit Wright's artistic vision, he had a rocky start in launching a mainstream publishing career. He was not only a politically radical writer in a nation that was often wary of radical political critiques, he was also a black writer in a country steeped in racism. Wright's second attempt at a novel, *Tarbaby's Dawn*, chronicles the story of a black adolescent boy coming of age in the South. Although several editors praised his ability to capture the rhythms of regional life, this manuscript too was repeatedly rejected by publishers who were not certain that Wright had yet perfected his craft. Maxim Lieber, Jack Conroy's literary agent, read both *Tarbaby's Dawn* and what was to become *Lawd Today!*, afterward telling Wright that he lacked a good understanding of how to construct a novel and was instead attempting to string together short episodes haphazardly into a book-length text.

Lieber's critiques—which Wright found unnecessarily harsh—may have been astute because Wright's initial mainstream success was to come as a writer of short fiction rather than as a novelist. In 1936 his short story "Big Boy Leaves Home," about a young man who witnesses the lynching of his best friend, had been published in *The New Caravan*, an anthology of short fiction. The major turning point in Wright's career came soon thereafter, at the close of 1937, when he learned that he had won a short-fiction contest sponsored by the prestigious *Story* magazine. Wright's enthusiasm for winning was slightly tarnished when word leaked that one of the judges, Sinclair Lewis, whose writing Wright had admired since his days in Memphis, had not liked his work. The other judges, however, were enthusiastic, choosing his work from more than five hundred entries. Wright was startled to learn that not only would he receive a five-hundred-dollar cash prize, but his story, "Fire and Cloud," would appear in *Story* magazine, and Harper & Brothers had agreed to publish a collection of four of his short stories.

The resulting collection, *Uncle Tom's Children*, initially appeared in 1938 and was expanded in 1940 to include an additional short story as well as a short autobiographical piece. It received rave reviews. Eleanor Roosevelt praised the book in a column in the *New York World–Telegram*, bringing it to the attention of many Americans who might not otherwise keep abreast of the latest literary news. Wright's stories, all set in the South, deal with the theme of racial oppression. As the title of the collection suggests, Wright's protagonists are not cringing, subservient African Americans, as in Harriet Beecher Stowe's 1852 fictional creation, "Uncle Tom." The next generation of blacks, Wright showed his readers, was finding ways to subvert the system of white supremacy, whether by fleeing, by fighting, or by protesting collectively. Protest, Wright implied, might ultimately be futile, but struggle for its own sake is portrayed as significant. These stories clearly bear the imprint of Wright's Communist training and his belief that black America's best chance to thwart racism would come through biracial organizing along class lines. But the stories do not read as political tracts, nor do they pose simplistic solutions to American racism. They are powerfully and elegantly written and generally considered to be among Wright's most successful works.

After the triumph of *Uncle Tom's Children*, Wright found himself in a different league. No longer could publishers quickly and easily dismiss his submissions. Buoyed by his success, he set about finding a literary agent who could help advance his career still further. Mary Folsom, whom Wright knew through their mutual affiliation with the Communist party, introduced him to her employer, Paul Reynolds, Jr., of the prestigious Paul Reynolds Literary Agency. The agency had represented the African-American poet Paul Laurence Dunbar and counted F. Scott Fitzgerald, George Bernard Shaw, and Willa Cather among its list of clients. Reynolds was impressed with Wright's talent and agreed to represent him, ultimately serving as his agent from 1938 until Wright's death in 1960.

The Reynolds family had deep Boston roots and claimed to have been descended from Paul Revere. Apparently the patrician Paul Reynolds, Jr., had relatively little in common with his new client, the self-educated black man who had clawed his way up from poverty and obscurity in Mississippi to the verge of literary fame. But the two men became close personal friends who for the next twenty-two years corresponded on a variety of issues, literary and otherwise. Their personal connection transcended not only differences in race and social class but also politics. Reynolds was conservative by temperament and leery of many of the strong indictments of the United States that were to flow from Wright's pen in the coming years. Nonetheless he conscientiously guided Wright in his transition from an obscure Communist poet to a major literary figure.

Without a doubt, Wright's success with *Uncle Tom's Children* sealed his reputation and in retrospect his fate. His gamble in moving to New York and turning down a permanent job in the post office had paid off. In 1938, at the age of thirty, he had almost arrived. Outwardly ever poised and confident, Wright seemed to take naturally to the new role he was beginning to assume, that of a well-known writer and public intellectual. During this period he became acquainted with many of the major African-American artists and intellectuals of his day as well as with a wide range of New York editors, critics, artists, and socialites. From this point on he had no shortage of dinner invitations. The trappings of celebrity must have been appealing to the man who had once been a half-starved, scantily educated boy from Mississippi. His success allowed him a sense of triumph against Granny who had tried to stifle her grandson's imagination, against the members of the black community who were more concerned about his immortal soul than his worldly ambitions, and against his white employers who seen him merely as a source of muscle rather than as an intellectual force to be reckoned with.

The richly textured and darkly imagined stories of *Uncle Tom's Children*, while nearly universally embraced by the critics, in Wright's estimation ultimately did not achieve their desired effect. He later surprised fans of his novellas when he speculated that in writing the earlier stories he had made an "awfully naive mistake." He worried that in writing these stories with sympathetic black protagonists who were persecuted and brutalized by a racist society, he had merely provided his white readers with an opportunity for catharsis. He became determined next time to take a more dramatic approach, to write something "so hard and deep that [his readers] would have to face it without the consolation of tears."

Craft and technique were important to Wright, who had self-consciously tutored himself since his days in Memphis by reading great works of literature and by creating his own writing exercises. He wrote prodigiously and consistently, as much for himself as for his publishers, a fact that is clear from the hundreds of unpublished pages of manuscript housed among his papers in the Beinecke Library at Yale University. As important as it was to him to perfect his skills as a writer, he never succumbed to what he saw as the wrongheaded indulgence of practicing art for its own sake. He saw himself consistently as a social activist, as someone who carried a perpetual burden of speaking for the oppressed, of giving voice to the experiences of people who because of racism, poverty, and isolation lacked either the ability or the platform to do so.

In some ways he was an unlikely spokesperson. There was much that Wright did not admire about his family, about the larger black community of his childhood, and about many of his fellow African Americans in the Communist party. In his autobiography, *Black Boy,* he freely criticized all three groups while portraying himself as immune to the foibles he described and as generally set apart from the individuals who should have comprised his community. But he regarded the pathologies he identified in those closest to him as the outgrowth of racism, poverty, and a hopeless environment. If racism were eradicated, he seems to suggest, the dynamics of life in the black community would also improve.

Wright did not take lightly the responsibilities that accompanied his newfound prominence. He strove to understand the intricacies of the social reality he hoped to capture and critique in his writing. Beginning with his days in Chicago, he immersed himself in the social sciences, taking full advantage of his proximity to the "Chicago School" of sociologists and anthropologists who were revolutionizing their disciplines at the same time he was trying to survive the depression. His first concrete connection to the community of social scientists at work in Chicago came, oddly enough, through Mary Wirth, the social worker assigned to his family when the self-reliant Wright felt compelled to ask for public assistance. Wirth's husband Louis was a sociologist well-known for his research on the formation of urban ghettos, a subject of obvious interest to Wright. It is a testament to his curiosity and self-confidence that he approached

Professor Wirth and asked him for a reading list, which he devoured. Wirth also introduced him to the prominent black sociologist Horace Cayton, who was to become a close friend and collaborator. Cayton immediately recognized Wright's aptitude as an amateur sociologist and in fact felt a deeper intellectual connection to Wright than he did to most professional social scientists. Cayton was not alone among academics in recognizing Wright's intellectual seriousness and talent. In the 1950s the African-American political scientist John A. Davis wrote to Wright saying, "The trouble with you as an important artist is that the social scientists have undoubtedly lost an important social scientist."

Wright was thrilled in June 1938 when the Works Progress Administration agreed to transfer him to the creative work section of the Federal Writers' Program. In his new assignment he was finally free to pursue his own creative projects. First on his agenda was a novel. Although Wright was still flushed with the critical triumph of *Uncle Tom's Children*, it must have bothered him that his two previous attempts at a novel had been unsuccessful. Now he was determined to depart from the formula he had established in his stories of writing sympathetically about Southern black victims of racial oppression. He wanted to break new ground both as an artist and a social critic.

While writing the novel, Wright lived in Brooklyn with Herbert and Jane Newton, friends from Chicago who had also relocated to New York. Although Herbert worked long hours as a party organizer, Jane was frequently at home with the couple's small children. She had long conversations with Wright about the plot of the book, passionately arguing with him about details she found implausible. Although Wright generally listened to his own internal voice rather than to the suggestions of his critics, whether his agent, his editors, or his friends, he did adopt at least one of Jane's suggestions.

She found it preposterous that Wright's protagonist could cut off a human head with a jacknife. Using a dead chicken as a prop, she convinced Wright that the job would require a hatchet. His final product, published in 1940 as *Native Son*, bears not only the stamp of some of her input but benefited from the happy, domestic routine that Wright enjoyed while living in the Newton home. Wright later recalled that their place was filled with "talks, rum, argument, politics, and laughter."

Wright did most of the writing for the novel over a period of four months, working out of inspiration and a desire to produce another book before his success with *Uncle Tom's Children* had faded from the memory of the literary establishment. The resulting story combined Communist party doctrine with Wright's interest in the social sciences. It is a fictionalized attempt to find an answer to a question posed throughout the social sciences: What is the impact of environment upon human development? He examined this question through the novel's protagonist, Bigger Thomas, a young man from the South Side of Chicago. In the opening scenes of the book, Bigger's mother orders him to kill a rat in the family's crowded kitchenette. When Bigger crushes the rat's skull, he foreshadows his own fate. Wright makes it clear that, like the rat, Bigger too is trapped in a hostile environment. His opportunities are limited, and he too is destined to be trampled by an indifferent society.

At the start of the novel, the reader learns that Bigger has been offered a job as a chauffeur for a prosperous white family, the Daltons. Mr. Dalton is a slumlord who has made his money by charging exorbitant rents to the residents of Bigger's neighborhood. Despite the dubious way he earns his living, Dalton fancies himself a philanthropist, donating Ping-Pong tables to the South Side Boys' Club and hiring this young man from the ghetto to be the family driver.

Wright in 1939, on the verge of literary fame. *(Library of Congress, photograph by Carl Van Vechten)*

Mary, his daughter, has become involved in the Communist party and is determined to be seen as anti-racist. She and her Communist boyfriend Jan embarrass Bigger with their familiarity and their inability to understand not only the racial divide but the barriers of education and social class that stand between them. Bigger is humiliated when they ask him to drive them to an African-American restaurant on the South Side of town, which they insist upon integrating. They force Bigger to eat with them, much to his chagrin.

The climax of the novel comes after Bigger drops off Jan after their night on the town, drives Mary home, and then helps the drunken young woman inside the house and into her bedroom. There is a moment of sexual attraction between the two young people as he helps her into bed, and he panics when her blind mother enters the room to check on her daughter. Terrified that he will be discovered inside Mary's bedroom, he panics. Attempting to quiet Mary, he smothers her with a pillow. After discovering that he has inadvertently killed her, he decapitates her body and burns it in the family's furnace. He later compounds this gruesome action when he rapes and murders his girlfriend Bessie. In the aftermath of these desperate and brutal actions, the local police hunt Bigger down like the rat in the apartment. He is captured and taken to prison, where he finds legal representation in the form of Boris Max, a Communist lawyer.

The character of Max pays homage to the Communist lawyers of the International Labor Defense organization, which had come to the aid of the Scottsboro Boys and other African Americans denied fair treatment by the legal system. Clarence Darrow, the famed lawyer who had been involved both with the Scopes Trial and later with a defense of the millionaire murderers Leopold and Loeb, may have also have been a source of inspiration for the character of Max. When Max tries to place the society that created Bigger on trial along with his defendant, arguing that Bigger is a product of his bleak environment, his argument falls on deaf ears, and Bigger receives the death penalty.

In October 1938 a draft of Wright's novel arrived on the desk of Ed Aswell, an editor at Harper & Brothers who was to become Wright's favorite editor and a close personal friend. Aswell liked the manuscript and immediately offered him a contract. In early 1939 Wright also received the welcome news that he had been awarded a prestigious Guggenheim Fellowship. It allowed him to resign his position with the Federal Writers' Project, and from that point onward he never received a regular paycheck. He would manage the remarkable feat of supporting himself and later his family on the proceeds from his writing. Soon Wright received even more astonishing news when Aswell informed him that the Book-of-the-Month Club was considering *Native Son* as one of their selections. The mail-order book club had 500,000 members in 1940, and about half that number generally purchased the monthly selection. Being chosen as a Book-of-the-Month Club selection would not only ensure large sales but would guarantee widespread publicity for the book.

Ultimately the club selected *Native Son* to become the first novel written by an African American to become a Book-of-the-Month selection. But the club made this historic decision on the condition that Wright agree to certain revisions. One was to pare some of Max's lengthy courtroom speeches, a change that had also been recommended by both Reynolds and Aswell. Most critics agree that this change strengthened the narrative power of the novel. But the other changes that the club's readers asked for were more significant. Nervous about the interracial sexual tension between Mary and Bigger, they asked Wright to tone down the scene between Bigger and Mary in her bedroom. In Wright's original version it was clear that the sexual attraction was mutual. Bigger "felt the sharp bones of her hip move in a hard and veritable grind" as he lifted her. In the final published version, however, Mary is more passive, and the implication that Bigger might become a rapist rather than a consensual lover is greater.

If Wright strongly objected to these changes, there is no trace of his protests in the historical record. In terms of book sales, he was certainly rewarded for his willingness to compromise. *Native Son* sold 215,000 copies within the first three weeks of publication, generating a firestorm of critical opinion. Initial reviews from the literary establishment sealed Wright's reputation as a major American novelist. In the pages of the *New Yorker*, Clifton Fadiman compared the book to Theodore Dreiser's *An American Tragedy*, an

evaluation that must have thrilled Wright who considered
Dreiser to be the greatest living American writer. In the
New Republic, Malcolm Cowley invoked John Steinbeck's
Pulitzer Prize–winning 1939 novel, *The Grapes of Wrath*,
in his affirmative review of *Native Son*. Writing in the *New
York Times*, Charles Poore lauded Wright's talent, saying
straightforwardly, "He knows how to tell a story." Some
voices of dissent also could be heard. Howard Mumford
Jones admitted the novel had an "uneven effect" on him.
In the *American Mercury*, Burton Rascoe was unmoved by
the praise lavished on the novel by others, declaring harshly
that "it is impossible to conceive of a novel's being worse."

By most accounts, Wright realized his intention to shock
his readers by forcing them to consider the impact of American racism not only on its direct victims but on society as a
whole. The vision he created was frightening. Critic Harry
Hansen said the novel smashed "like a big fist through the
windows of our complacent lives." Readers were unable to
respond to the book's protagonist with the nearly unani-
mous sympathy that his beleaguered black characters in
Uncle Tom's Children had evoked. Most black critics hailed
Wright's achievements at least publicly, and his book was
praised in the pages of *Opportunity* and the *Crisis* among
other prominent black publications. Some writers, like
Langston Hughes, were privately more ambivalent about
the book. Wright's explanation that Bigger was merely a
product of his environment proved less than satisfying to
many black readers who worried that Wright's brutal black
protagonist reinforced black stereotypes and damaged the
burgeoning struggle for civil rights by inflaming white fears
rather than eliciting white sympathy. Writing in the *Baltimore Afro-American*, Lillian Johnson worried that "the
book could do a great deal of harm."

Wright's colleagues in the Communist party also had a
mixed reception for the book. The party wanted to support

the creative efforts of one of its best-known writers, but many party members criticized Wright for not properly touting the party line. *Native Son*, after all, does not extol the revolutionary potential of the proletariat. Furthermore, the Communist characters in the book are presented as sympathetic but flawed rather than as unambiguously heroic. Between April 23 and May 21, 1940, *New Masses* printed a series of responses to the novel, offering both praise and damns.

Wright anticipated a mixed response, knowing as he sent the final draft of the manuscript off to Aswell that middle-class African Americans and his comrades in the Communist party might find much in the novel to unsettle them. Regardless of the criticism he received, the publication of *Native Son* transformed Wright into a cultural figure who could not be ignored. Writing in *Dissent* more than twenty years later, Irving Howe declared that "The day *Native Son* arrived, American culture was changed forever." Whether or not readers could, like Boris Max, tap into unknown recesses of empathy for the novel's brutal protagonist, they had to engage with the specter of Bigger Thomas after his arrival on the American cultural landscape. Similarly, Wright's literary heirs have had to grapple with the meaning of *Native Son* and in some way to juxtapose their own creative works against the bleak universe Wright created. More than three generations of readers who have confronted Bigger have been forced to confront Wright's burning questions about collective culpability for the desperate actions of those who are excluded from American largesse. After Bigger's arrival, Wright was left to make sense of the paradoxical fact that he had transformed his long-standing grudge against American racism into a product that was to earn him fame and financial success.

CHAPTER FOUR

Marriage

_✍_ When it was becoming clear to Wright that he would succeed in his work, he decided it was time to put his personal life in order. At the age of thirty he consciously set out to find a wife.

Wright was generally reticent in talking about his personal life, choosing to keep his romantic attachments private. In the published version of his autobiography, he recalls having erotic fantasies about an elder's wife while attending church with his grandmother as a child, and he confesses to a couple of casual sexual encounters during his late adolescence and early adulthood. But he makes no public admissions about any lasting affairs of the heart. Earlier drafts of the manuscript for _Black Boy_ reveal that he had adolescent crushes on two of his classmates, Carlotta Metcalf and Birdie Graves, but he worshiped them from afar, preferring the fantasy of these young women to concrete knowledge of them. When it came to romance, he recalled, "as soon as the ideal turned into reality, I would have none of it." He was too focused on his goal of leaving Mississippi to allow himself to be drawn into a lasting attachment.

Wright had no shortage of female admirers. People were drawn to him. He carried himself with dignity and confidence, successfully masking inner uncertainties he might have felt. He was also an enthusiastic conversationalist and a good listener who put people at ease with his ready laugh. Many people who met Wright after reading his strong, angry prose were surprised at how personable and warm he was in person. Adding to his allure was the fact that he was generally thought to be quite handsome. He had a strong profile and a penetrating gaze that was softened by the enigmatic half-smile he often wore. As a young man living in Chicago, he capitalized on these charms and had a number of discreet affairs. Establishing himself as a writer, however, rather than finding love, remained his driving preoccupation.

In these casual romances Wright found himself willing to break one of the most intense taboos of his Southern childhood: the proscription on interracial sexual relationships. Among members and sympathizers of the Communist party, romances between black and white members were a common and intensely personal manifestation of the party's commitment to anti-racism. Yet even in this atmosphere of official tolerance, tensions surfaced. Most interracial marriages among party members were between black men and white women, seldom the other way around, a fact that led to some ambivalence about the implications of these relationships.

Wright's good friends Herbert and Jane Newton followed the pattern of a black man married to a white woman, but they also provided him with a positive example of an interracial romance. Eventually he witnessed the closeness of their relationship firsthand while living in their home. But these newer models of interracial love could not have completely displaced Wright's earlier education on the subject. He and other transplanted Southerners must have grappled with the lingering effects of their Jim Crow indoctrination both inside as well as outside the bedroom.

In the segregated South, sexual encounters between white men and black women were extremely common. These

generally surreptitious liaisons were clouded by an invari-
ably uneven balance of power and a general tolerance of the
rape of black women. In contrast, relationships between
white women and black men were banned in the South.
Even the vaguest suggestion of interracial sexual longing between white women and black men could have disastrous
consequences. Acting on these desires often proved to be
deadly. Wright must have remembered his teenage terror
after he discovered that an acquaintance had been lynched
for allegedly having sexual relations with a white prostitute.
When he moved to Chicago, he had to work to overcome his
discomfort about being in close physical proximity to white
women whose very presence conjured up associations with
violent death.

Wright must have been aware of the symbolic signifi-
cance of even his most casual affair with a white woman. By
openly defying one of the crowning principles of white supremacy, he was again resisting the race rules that had governed his behavior throughout his childhood. In choosing
white sexual partners, however, he also risked raising the
ire of some black women who understandably believed that
a member of their own race would be a more appropriate
partner for this up-and-coming young writer. Even in these
very intimate decisions, Wright would have been faced with
the perennial conflict between his own needs and desires
and his sense of obligation to the black community.

Wright's relationships during his Chicago years tended
to be brief, transient affairs. Thus he felt relatively free from
the burden of having to scrutinize the political implications
of these encounters. He was, after all, not yet contemplat-
ing marriage. Whether or not he was troubled by any of the
wider moral implications of these relationships is unknown.
Joyce Gourfain, one of his white lovers, was purportedly
quite besotted with Wright. He was much more casual in

his attachment to her. He was no stranger to inequalities in romantic attachments, but in spite of his eloquence he was surprisingly inept in navigating the dangerous terrain of unrequited love. During his childhood he had developed an emotional steeliness that served as a defense mechanism, a way to keep his stern grandmother and fragile mother at arm's length so they could not thwart his future plans with their demands or their neediness. This posture of carefully cultivated aloofness followed him into adulthood, influencing both his romantic relationships and his friendships.

Wright's most documented relationship with a woman during his Chicago years was his friendship with Margaret Walker. He met Walker in 1935 when they worked together on the Federal Writers' Project. Seven years Wright's junior, she had moved to Chicago to attend Northwestern University. She had been born into a middle-class black family in Alabama; her father was a minister and her mother a music teacher. She had enjoyed a far more sheltered and comfortable childhood than Wright. What drew them together, then, was not their common Southern background but their shared dream of becoming successful writers. Both were members of the South Side Writers' Group. In that setting and beyond they spent many hours sharing their work and talking about the peculiar problems faced by African-American artists.

Walker was extremely girlish, both in appearance and demeanor, when she met the worldlier Wright. She weighed less than a hundred pounds and was flat-chested. In keeping with her respectable origins she dressed fastidiously and conservatively in pleated skirts and pearl earrings, offering the impression of a precocious schoolgirl. She was immediately taken with Wright, and though she never admitted it, observers were certain that she was in love with him. Wright initially welcomed her friendship, but it was clear from the outset that he did not share her intensity of feeling about the relationship.

Walker was buoyed by Wright's early successes—both because of her affection for him and because she hoped to follow in his literary footsteps. When he decided to pursue his writing career in New York, Walker applauded his decision, telling him that he would be wasting his talent if he stayed behind to work at the post office. For the first two years after he moved to New York, they corresponded. Walker filled him in on the local news, congratulated him on his growing success, and confided in him about her own creative attempts. She also faithfully sent Wright clippings related to the trial of Robert Nixon, a black man from Chicago who had confessed to killing and raping several women. The details of Nixon's trial provided Wright with important inspiration as he wrote *Native Son*. Through the years, many of Wright's friends complained that he did not always answer letters, but he was careful to keep in touch with Walker largely out of gratitude for her help with his novel. She was thrilled by the attention and set herself up as a mediator between him and his Chicago friends. She was also quick to pass on local gossip, informing him on several occasions that his former comrades were jealous of his literary success.

Walker was caught in the impossible situation of being hopelessly in love with someone who could not return her affection in kind. Her letters to Wright gently and repeatedly probed the issues of sexuality and romantic attachments between men and women, as if in broaching these subjects she hoped to inspire Wright into a confession. Although Wright was impressed by her shining intelligence, he was also startled by her naiveté. She and Wright never shared any physical intimacy throughout their three-year-long friendship, but she let herself hope that their connection was stronger than mere friendship. Due to her sheltered upbringing and conservative values, when she met Wright she was not only sexually inexperienced but also unschooled in sexual subjects. Dangerously, she was prone to fill in the gaps in her understanding with an overactive imagination. She was also known for her willingness to share her speculations out loud.

Walker's youthful enthusiasm and her openness about many of her feelings put her temperamentally at odds with Wright. Although outwardly gregarious, Wright used his outgoing personality as a shield to protect the privacy of his thoughts. He chose to reveal his interior life only through his writing, not in casual conversation. He did not enjoy being the object of gossip or speculation, and as long as he maintained a correspondence with Walker he knew she would distribute tidbits of information about him among his Chicago acquaintances. He may have spoken to Walker about his concerns because in several letters she told him earnestly that she was trying not to gossip. Her attempts to hold her tongue ultimately failed, however, and as a result she lost Wright's friendship.

In June 1939, Walker traveled to New York to attend the Third American Writers' Conference, a two-day gathering of leftist writers. Both Wright and Langston Hughes, who had encouraged Walker in her writing, were scheduled to attend. While there she also hoped to find a publisher for the novel she had just completed. Like most of her friends in Chicago who were trying to launch writing careers, Walker was barely scraping by. She had to borrow money for her train ticket to get to New York. When she arrived, Wright met her at the station. She confided in him about her financial woes. Always empathetic on the subject of money, Wright reassured her and lent her enough cash to enable her to live comfortably for the rest of the trip. He also arranged accommodations for her during the visit: she was to stay at the Harlem apartment of the journalist Marvel Cooke.

Although Wright willingly took responsibility for Walker's well-being during her visit, having her in New York put him on edge. She was not as interested as he thought she should be in the conference itself. He treated her cordially but with a degree of distance. They ate most of their meals together along with other conference attendees, including Ralph Ellison, but Wright chose not to accompany Walker to a Broadway show that she had invited him to. Always looking for explanations of the unsatisfactory limitations of her relationship with Wright, she seized on the idea that he might be homosexual or bisexual. She became concerned about the precise nature of his close relationships with Ted Ward and Langston Hughes and intimated as much to Wright. This seems to have been the final straw in their already strained relationship; he did not wish to become the subject of more gossip and speculation, especially not about his sexual orientation. Wright asked to speak to Walker in private and told her that their friendship was over. She should pack her bags and go back to Chicago. When she asked him why, he told her to examine her conscience for an answer. Walker wrote him a tortured letter of apology, acknowledging that she had been a "foolish and giddy girl who rather indiscreetly had talked too much." Wright was apparently unmoved by her pain; he never spoke to her again.

After she returned to Chicago, Margaret Walker received a postcard, which Langston Hughes sent to her and to some of their friends, playfully commenting on what had happened in a short poem entitled "Epic":

Margaret Walker is a talker
When she came to town
What she said put Ted in bed
And turned Dick upside down.

His relationship with Walker was not the only one that Wright ended abruptly. He found emotional scenes exhausting, and he did whatever he could to avoid interpersonal drama. Although he loved to argue about art and politics, he could not bear disputes about what he regarded as petty things. When he decided to end a relationship, he ended it. There would be no painful negotiations. In 1938, convinced that it was time for him to marry, he somewhat impulsively proposed to Marion Sawyer, the daughter of his landlady. She accepted, and invitations were sent out. But he recoiled when the blood tests needed for a marriage license revealed that his bride-to-be had congenital syphilis. He made an abrupt and final break with her and tried to limit the spread of rumors about his engagement and aborted marriage plans by denying everything or refusing to speak of it. Sawyer's mother responded to the crisis by sending out postcards announcing that her daughter's nuptials had been postponed indefinitely.

Sawyer was at least the second woman Wright had proposed marriage to. The first was the daughter of a middle-class African-American woman from Brooklyn. Her father, leery of Wright's prospects to be able to support his daughter, refused to consent to the match. Being spurned by the family was probably humiliating to Wright. When he was around members of the black bourgeoisie who were university educated, he was uncomfortably reminded of his scant formal education. He feared that no level of current accomplishment could erase the memories of his unhappy childhood or convince some black professionals to regard him as a social equal. Nonetheless these two relationships also suggest that Wright initially planned to marry a black woman and made conscious attempts to find someone suitable. The next time he proposed marriage, however, it was to a white woman.

Among Wright's female friends at this time were two alluring but temperamentally very different white women: Dhimah Rose Meadman and Ellen Poplowitz. Both were from Jewish families and were members of the Communist party, but their similarities ended there. Meadman was tall with dark hair and dramatic features. She capitalized on her exotic appearance, sometimes falsely telling people she was from Egypt, thus distinguishing herself from many other party members whose origins were in Eastern Europe. Not only was she deliberately misleading about her place of birth, she also gave various birth dates ranging from 1900 to 1907. Although she was reluctant to admit it, she was probably several years older than Wright.

Meadman had trained as a ballet dancer in Russia, and when Wright met her she was operating a modern dance studio in New York. She was divorced with a small child and lived with her mother in the fashionable Sugar Hill neighborhood of Harlem. As a dancer she carried herself regally. In contrast to Margaret Walker, Meadman was sophisticated and composed, a woman of the world. Wright's closest friend at the time, Ralph Ellison, privately worried that she was actually too cosmopolitan for his friend, whose manners and bearing struck the always stylish Ellison as somewhat crude. Her creativity and artistic temperament were appealing to Wright who, as a still loyal party member, was relieved that they had common political beliefs as well.

Ellen Poplowitz, the other rival for Wright's affection, was also a loyal party member whose parents had immigrated to the United States from Poland. Born in 1912, she was four years Wright's junior. She was petite with dark hair, hazel eyes, and an attractive face delicately sprinkled with freckles. She lacked Meadman's air of worldly sophistication due to her youthful appearance and to the fact that she had never traveled abroad. In contrast to the theatrical Dhimah

Rose Meadmen, Ellen Poplowitz was pragmatic and earnest. Devoted to the party, she led the Fulton Street branch in Brooklyn. Just as during his Chicago years Wright placed his creative work above romance, when Poplowitz met Wright in April 1939 romance was the farthest thing from her mind. Her party work came first.

As different as these two women were, Wright was drawn to them both. As he began to think seriously about proposing to yet a third woman, he realized that the field had narrowed to these two contenders. Although he had initial reservations about marrying a white woman, he was determined not to let what he saw as a misplaced sense of race loyalty shape this very private decision. For Wright, transcending racism meant finding personal freedom to do and to love as he wished. He would not let social expectations from either the white or the black community cloud his own judgment as he made—once again—the decision to marry.

After he made his peace with the idea of interracial marriage, it was important to him that the woman he chose would be able gracefully and willingly to handle the hardships that such a relationship would involve. In choosing Wright, Meadman or Poplowitz would be volunteering to sample firsthand some of the adversities associated with racial prejudice and would have to surrender some of her white privilege. Even in Manhattan, African Americans could not be assured service at just any hotel or restaurant, and entry to a new place was always accompanied by a measure of apprehension. Although each woman would certainly have experienced anti-Semitism, crossing the racial divide in this way would bring her face to face with a far more virulent form of prejudice than she had experienced before.

Almost in spite of herself, Ellen Poplowitz found herself drawn to Richard Wright, who began attending branch meetings just so he could hear Ellen speak. Soon she too

found excuses to seek him out, frequently dropping by the
Newton household where Wright was staying, claiming that
party business had brought her there. Soon the two found
themselves embroiled in a romance, the intensity of which
surprised them. Whether or not Wright formally proposed
marriage, the subject of such a union certainly came up in
conversation. Ever thoughtful and slow to act, Ellen was
reluctant to enter into this relationship impetuously. This
stood in stark contrast to her suitor, who had now spoken of
marriage to at least three women in fewer than two years.
Ellen knew that marriage to a black man would prove unsettling to her family and that in choosing to marry Wright she
might very well end her relationship with her opinionated
and temperamental mother. She needed some time to think
through the implications of this choice. At the very least, she
wanted time to devise the best way of breaking the news to
her family. After an intense conversation with Wright about
the possibility of marrying, she left for her summer job as a
counselor at a summer camp sponsored by the party.

During her time away from Wright, Ellen became aware
of the depth of her feelings for him. When the summer ended
she returned to New York and moved out of her parents'
home in Brooklyn and into a rented room in Manhattan. Her
independence thus declared, she enthusiastically arranged a
meeting with Wright to tell him that she had made up her
mind. Without reservation she wanted to marry him. She
was floored when he coolly informed her that in her absence
he had made other plans. He now wanted to spend his life
with Dhimah.

Wright had always been attracted to Dhimah, and he
felt rebuffed by what he saw as Ellen's unforgivable hesita-
tion to marry him. Much as he had with Margaret Walker,
he made an abrupt break with Ellen and stubbornly carried
out his wedding plans. On August 12, 1939, Wright married

Dhimah Meadman in an Episcopal church in Harlem. Ralph Ellison and his first wife Rose served as the only witnesses. Wright made no attempt to publicize the marriage, news of which reached his friends slowly, if at all.

Shortly after the wedding, the couple left the city for a several-month stay in the Mohegan Colony, a retreat that had been founded by anarchists in the 1920s in Westchester County. When the Wrights arrived, Mohegan was home to bohemians and political dissidents of various persuasions. The tranquility of the rural environment was soothing to the newlyweds, who enjoyed their isolation. Wright, however, had to get used to living with Peter, Dhimah's young son, and her mother Eda, who seemed to accompany her daughter everywhere.

After royalties from *Native Son* began to bolster the balance in Wright's bank account, the family decided to relocate to an even more exotic writer's retreat—Cuernevaca, Mexico. Wright had long desired to spend some time outside the United States, and he admired Dhimah in part because she was cosmopolitan and had traveled. He knew that seeing more of the world was a necessary part of his education as a writer. The couple rented a luxurious villa complete with a swimming pool in an area where many American expatriates and vacationers lived. This time Dhimah was accompanied not only by her mother and her son but also by her pianist. Thus the young Marxist couple found themselves living in luxury and accompanied by an entourage, an unforeseen set of circumstances for the once chronically underprivileged Wright.

For a time they were happy in their new surroundings, and Wright experienced a welcome reprieve from American-style racism. But as a novice traveler Wright soon suffered the effects of culture shock. He found the local people primitive and dull, and he was appalled by the overwhelming poverty he encountered when he left his posh, tourist-friendly enclave. And he soon felt isolated by the absence of American radio broadcasts and newspapers. He had to rely on his friend Ralph Ellison to update him about the buzz *Native Son* was generating. Ellison flatteringly compared the book to the Bible, telling him "it seems to hold *some* kind of satisfaction for all." Although generous with his praise for his mentor's talents, Ellison did not spare Wright from the knowledge that many readers were ambivalent if not outright hostile to Wright's efforts. "*Native Son*," he told Wright, "shook the Harlem section to its foundation and some of the rot it has brought up is painful to smell." Letters like these increased Wright's feelings of isolation, and he became frustrated by his inability to experience at firsthand the fallout from the publication of his first novel.

To make matters worse, his relationship with Dhimah began to deteriorate during this Mexican sojourn. The couple had been married for seven months when they arrived in Cuernavaca. After a stay of slightly less than three months, their marriage was all but over. Wright found it difficult to share a space with a noisy young child who distracted him from his work. He was also somewhat ill at ease in his luxurious surroundings where the family was waited on by an army of servants. His wife, however, seemed well suited to their new surroundings, and Wright began to disdain her as being too free with money, spoiled, and bourgeois. He was particularly offended by the harsh and indifferent way she treated the servants. Ever uncomfortable with intense emotional scenes, he was appalled to discover that his new wife was prone to what he regarded as temper tantrums. Not long after their arrival, Dhimah was stung by a scorpion and had to receive a number of injections to counteract the poison. Wright, however, was so soured on the relationship that he could hardly conjure up sympathy for her pain, later tell-

Taken during Wright's only return visit to Mississippi, in 1940, this photo shows, from left, his cousin Louis Wright, his father Nathaniel, Richard, and his uncles Rias Wright and Solomon Wright. *(Yale Collection of American Literature, Beinecke Rare Book and Manuscript Library)*

ing friends that he had some admiration for the "beast that stood up to her."

When they departed Mexico, they did so separately. Dhimah and her entourage headed to New York while Wright decided on a journey into his past, making the only return visit of his life to Mississippi. Even if their marriage had been a happy one, it would have been impossible for the couple to travel together inside the segregated South. Wright boarded a train in Mexico City, preparing himself for the humiliations in store for him when he crossed the border. When the train entered Texas, the passengers were relocated to segregated cars, and customs officials viewed Wright warily, questioning him about his portable typewriter and the books he carried with him. With his expensive clothing and his cosmopolitan air, he had lost his ability to blend safely into the landscape of Jim Crow.

Upon his arrival in Mississippi he was newly assaulted by the indignities imposed on the region's black residents as he tried to find restaurants and sanitary restroom facilities. Although his socioeconomic status had changed since his deprived childhood, as a black man he was still governed by local customs and by the signs designating inferior "colored" facilities. While in Mississippi he saw his father for the last time. By now Nathaniel Wright had returned to sharecropping, and Wright traveled to the countryside outside Natchez to awkwardly become reacquainted with his father, a man in overalls who seemed beaten by life and who had no way to comprehend his son's very different existence. Wright must have noticed his own striking physical resemblance to his father, and as he contemplated ending his own marriage he may have taken time to reflect on the way his father had abruptly left his mother for another woman without ever demonstrating any regret.

Dhimah, hopeful that she and Wright would reconcile, asked the Ellisons to share an apartment with her in New York. Lured by the prospect of inexpensive rent and unaware of the permanent rift in her relationship with Wright, Ralph and Rose Ellison readily agreed to the arrangement. Meanwhile Wright left Mississippi for North Carolina where he was scheduled to begin collaborating with the Pulitzer Prize–winning playwright Paul Green on a stage version of *Native Son.* Weeks later, when Wright found his way back to New York, he did not join Dhimah and the Ellisons. Instead he moved back into the Newton household. Staying with his long-established pattern of ending relationships abruptly, he visited Dhimah only once. In his mind their marriage was over, and he had no interest in lengthy emotional conversations. He filed for divorce in the summer of 1940. In the future he spoke of the marriage only reluctantly, if at all, even to his closest friends.

Soon afterward Ellen Poplowitz dropped by the Newton home to see Wright. They were both overcome by emotion, flying into each other's arms. Ellen too now moved into the Newton household, and within seven months she would become Wright's second wife. When the couple wed on March 12, 1941, Wright followed his usual pattern of secrecy about his private life. He did not even tell his closest friend, Ellison, about the wedding. No family from either side attended the ceremony, a civil service held in Coytesville, New Jersey. The marriage was witnessed by Abraham Aaron, Wright's Chicago friend who had introduced him to the John Reed Club, and Benjamin Davis, Jr., a prominent black Communist.

Wright must have felt some embarrassment about his checkered romantic past—one abruptly canceled wedding, one divorce, and now a second marriage to a white woman, all within the space of a few years' time. Even to his closest friends, Wright was reluctant to speak about the difficulties that accompanied interracial marriage. Venting in his diary, he railed against those who criticized him, claiming he did not set out to marry a "white" woman but rather a woman he loved. Nevertheless he and Ellen were clearly happy in the private world they created. They left the Newton household and moved into their own three-room apartment in Brooklyn. There Wright, a competent cook, began teaching his new wife some basic culinary techniques. The two enjoyed cozy evenings together dining on their creations and chatting about books. Like Wright, Ellen was a voracious reader who enjoyed talking about literature with her new husband. At his suggestion, she began reading Dreiser and soon agreed with her husband that he was indeed one of the greatest living American writers.

Although she had a lively intelligence and was a dedicated Communist who had adeptly managed a wide variety of party responsibilities, Ellen appeared to be content to live in the shadow of her prominent husband. Whereas Dhimah had her own creative aspirations, which consumed most of her energies, Ellen was willing to devote much of her life to aiding Wright in his work. In fact, for tax reasons Wright officially made Ellen his secretary, paying her a set salary for tasks such as typing and answering correspondence. The couple thrived under this arrangement. Wright enjoyed the pleasant domesticity of their early life together. In addition to becoming an excellent cook, Ellen learned how to knit, making ties for her new husband. Wright could not resist cooing about her homemaking accomplishments to his friend, the poet and experimental filmmaker Willard Maas, describing her early attempts at knitting as a "masterpiece of tangled whirl."

Their happiness was marred by Ellen's mother's refusal to approve of the marriage. Wright was adamant, however, that nothing tarnish the "peace and love" that existed in their home. For a time mother and daughter were estranged, lacking the tools to reconcile in the face of their mutual disappointments. Rose Poplowitz could not abide her daughter's choice of a husband, and Ellen was crushed by her mother's intolerance. But after Ellen learned that she was pregnant, her mother was no longer content to stay away. They must find a way to make peace. Although Ellen loved her, she found her mother excitable and prone to emotional arguments. The Wrights agreed that Rose Poplowitz could visit the couple only if she restrained herself. Wright could not abide hearing harsh words uttered in his presence, and he certainly did not like to see Ellen upset. For his part, Wright treated his mother-in-law with civility, adopting a falsely jovial voice when he spoke to her on the telephone.

Things were not perfect between them, but considering how strongly Rose had objected to her daughter's interracial union, the fact that the three managed to make peace at all was remarkable.

Julia Wright was born on April 15, 1942, and the first few years of her life were among Wright's happiest. He and Ellen fussed over the tiny baby, monitoring every sneeze and frown and keeping a careful eye on her when visitors entered their home. Wright doted on his little girl, read to her, and attempted to see the world through her eyes. He felt every racial slight, every hostile glance, every extended stare that assaulted their family's happiness more acutely for Julia's sake. Like African-American parents throughout history, he dreaded the moment when Julia would become aware of American racism and conscious of the limits that society would seek to impose on her life chances. Even though he lived in relative affluence in the most cosmopolitan city in the United States, Wright worried about his daughter's future. He could not shake off a streak of melancholy even during the magical first years of his daughter's life.

Although Ellen was Julia's primary caregiver, Wright also took a strong interest in raising Julia and in pampering her mother when she needed it, confiding in his diary that he found his wife to be "lovely and strange and helpless sometimes." The family hired a maid to help with household chores, but Wright too took on a share of the domestic responsibilities, particularly in the kitchen. He was not only an able cook but also a curious eater. Although he loved greens and cornbread, he was not particularly nostalgic about most of the Southern food of his childhood. He suffered from occasional stomach problems when he ate unfamiliar foods, nonetheless he took advantage of the wide variety of cuisine available in New York City and was willing to try food from around the world. He often cooked for Ellen and Julia as well as for visitors like the sociologist Horace Cayton. He particularly enjoyed baking homemade bread.

Shortly after Julia's birth, the family accepted the invitation of the writer and editor George Davis to move into his enormous Victorian house near the Brooklyn Bridge at 7 Middagh Street. Davis was the author of one novel and was better known as the literary editor for a series of magazines including *Vanity Fair* and *Harper's Bazaar.* Anais Nin described his Brooklyn home as a "museum of Americana," cluttered with lamps, clocks, and heavy furniture covered with lace doilies. He had converted it into a bohemian space for artists to live, and W. H. Auden and Carson McCullers among others once called this place home. The residents had wild parties that involved binge drinking and sexual experimentation. The Wrights resided on a private floor in the house and did not fully participate in the free-flowing atmosphere of what Davis came to describe as "our menagerie." Wright befriended everyone in the house and endeavored to remain tolerant of the exuberant atmosphere and openly homosexual behavior of many of the residents and guests. He could not help but admire this atmosphere of complete acceptance, and he found the alternative lifestyles of many of the residents fascinating but also at times excessive. Although he admired McCullers's tremendous talent as a writer, he came to abhor her drinking habits and her sometimes erratic behavior, and he and Ellen decided they needed to raise Julia in a calmer setting.

Even after they left the Davis house, Julia's life was far from ordinary. Her parents knew many of the bohemian white writers and intellectuals who resided in New York, and Wright maintained close relationships with many of the leading African-American thinkers of the day. The social anthropologist St. Clair Drake and his wife Liz frequently volunteered to baby-sit little Julia. Horace Cayton was a frequent visitor in the Wright home. Lawrence Reddick, curator of the New York Public Library's Schomburg Collection of materials related to the African-American experience, was also a close friend as was the renowned sociologist E. Franklin Frazier. During this period Wright began to frame his understanding of the black experience in the United States within the larger historical frameworks of the African Diaspora and the struggle against racism and colonialism throughout the globe. This outlook was encouraged in part by his friendship with C. L. R. James, a Marxist intellectual from Trinidad who moved to the United States in 1938, the same year he published his magisterial history of the Haitian revolution, *Black Jacobins*. These friendships with scholars underscored Wright's belief that fiction could serve a function similar to that of an academic study in documenting and explaining the black experience.

Wright was among the most famous and sought after members of his illustrious group of acquaintances. *Native Son* had already sealed his reputation as one of the most prominent American black writers. His international reputation was growing too, and his star would only continue to rise after the 1945 publication of his autobiography *Black Boy*. His prominence earned him numerous invitations, but Wright was often irked to discover that his less famous African-American friends seemed to be less welcome than he at many of these gatherings. Fame, he began to discover, had its drawbacks. Some of his friends began asking to borrow money, many because they vastly overestimated his wealth. Although his earnings from *Native Son* were impressive, much of the money had been swallowed up in taxes and fees to his agent. Nonetheless Wright obliged his friends as often as he was able.

Of course he was delighted that his work was well received, but he began to feel the strain from the constantly ringing telephone that interrupted his work and the speaking invitations that distracted him from his writing agenda. As he adjusted to his status as a literary celebrity, he treasured his family life even more. He needed a sanctuary where he could escape from the outside world. He and Ellen decided that they should buy a home they could call their own, an undertaking they knew would be a complicated one for their interracial family.

Throughout the United States in the 1940s, the vast majority of African-American homeowners lived in all-black neighborhoods. Because of overt prejudice as well as a fear that the presence of black neighbors would damage property values, whites tended to resist black incursions into what they regarded as their neighborhoods. Local residents were generally aided by realtors and by banks that actively discriminated against would-be black home buyers, limiting their ability to buy properties and obtain mortgages in predominantly white areas. When African Americans managed to break through the restrictive barriers designed to keep them out of particular neighborhoods, their white neighbors often responded with violence or threats. If intimidation failed, "white flight" set in as white residents abandoned their homes for racially exclusive enclaves elsewhere. Although New York was notable for a relative degree of racial tolerance, Wright, like African Americans everywhere, would have difficulty purchasing a home in a neighborhood of his choosing.

Buying property in Harlem was out of the question. Wright had gotten to know the neighborhood intimately while writing for the *Daily Worker*, and he had many friends and acquaintances who lived there. Throughout the time he lived in New York, he traveled to Harlem regularly to get his hair cut, and he loved the easy conversations that sprang up in the all-male environment of the black barbershop. But he resented the idea of living in a poor neighborhood where he would be forced to pay higher prices for basic necessities and where his daughter would have to attend what he regarded as inferior schools. As a black man, however, even a successful and famous one, he knew that he would have to act strategically in order to secure a mortgage to buy a home in a white area.

He and Ellen decided that Greenwich Village in lower Manhattan was their ideal neighborhood. Since the turn of the twentieth century, the area had been associated with bohemian lifestyles and had been home to a variety of writers, artists, and musicians. The Wrights hoped they might find a greater degree of racial tolerance there than in many of the more staid New York neighborhoods. They also admired the neighborhood's school system. When they located a property they wished to purchase at 13 Charles Street, their lawyer Jacob Salzman warned them—as they feared—that Wright would find it all but impossible to secure a mortgage for it. They were afraid to try to purchase the home in Ellen's name because they figured that a female buyer might also attract too much scrutiny.

In order to conceal their identities, the Wrights set up a dummy corporation, the Richelieu Company, which would seek to buy the property on their behalf. Using this guise, Salzman managed to secure a mortgage for them that covered $8,000 of the $18,000 purchase price. The rest of the money would be paid in cash and by a second mortgage that Paul Reynolds, Wright's agent, helped him secure using his future book contracts as collateral. Thus they managed to subvert the racist real estate system, but even in progressive Greenwich Village they could not avoid racism. When the neighbors discovered the identity of the new owner of 13 Charles Street, they quickly raised $20,000 to purchase the house, hoping to tempt the Wrights to take the quick profit and abandon the idea of living in the neighborhood. Wearily, Wright and his wife turned down their offer, and Wright set his jaw and prepared to fight yet another battle against American racism. Although purchasing the home was a bittersweet experience, they could now breathe a sigh of relief. They were happy together, and they had found a new home.

CHAPTER FIVE

Fame

و‚ After the publication of *Native Son*, Wright was financially capable of devoting himself completely to his craft. For an aspiring writer of fiction to transform his art from a hobby to an occupation is a rare accomplishment. For this once chronically disadvantaged African-American boy from Mississippi to do so was nothing short of miraculous. It appeared that Wright had assumed his new role gracefully. From an early age he had been determined to succeed, and part of him had never doubted his ability to recreate himself, to assume a way of life far different from the one he had been born into. But his success did not close the yawning gap he often felt between his own private experiences and the lives of others around him. Nor did it satisfy his lifelong inner cravings to be more, to see more, to do more. He was at root melancholy, alienated, and restless. Although the fruits of his success brought a much needed source of distraction, his fundamental nature was unchanged. His relationship with his wife and daughter soothed him and made him feel more connected to humanity, but at times he felt far away from even their love. In a journal he kept in 1945 he cried out, "Oh, God, how lonely I am with this burden of consciousness! If only there were supportive minds about me, kindred feelings."

Looking at Wright's life from the outside, his friends and acquaintances would likely have had trouble identifying him as a lonely man. Always charming, his company was prized. He had no shortage of invitations or correspondents, and his literary work would never again inspire as much praise and attention as it attracted during the World War II years. Yet despite the success of *Uncle Tom's Children* and the triumph of *Native Son,* Wright knew the sting of rejection. His first two novels had been rejected by every publisher he had sent them to. It was a novelty when people began to seek him out, when he was no longer forced to be tirelessly proactive, endlessly banging on the doors of mainstream publishing.

Many in the theater community were immediately struck by the dramatic possibilities of *Native Son.* Wright's agent, Paul Reynolds, had inquiries from several parties interested in producing a play based on the novel. Wright's friend from Chicago, the playwright Ted Ward, and the internationally famous actor and singer Paul Robeson, expressed an interest early on in adapting the novel for the stage. Wright and Ward had long been on friendly terms, beginning with their mutual involvement in the Chicago John Reed Club. Ward had had some success too. His most famous play, *Big White Fog,* about a black family struggling to survive during the depression was produced the same year that *Native Son* appeared. Of course Robeson's stature as an African-American actor and singer was unparalleled. Wright surely took seriously their interest in adapting the novel. Whether or not he felt any obligation to give preference to collaborating with other black artists is unknown. Ultimately, however, he granted the rights for a stage production to the white actor and producer John Houseman.

In 1936 Houseman had become the director of the Federal Negro Theater in Harlem. Wright, who had been briefly

involved with the Chicago counterpart, had become familiar with Houseman's work at that time and was particularly
impressed with his production of *Macbeth*, performed by
an all-black cast and directed by Orson Welles. Since then
Houseman and Welles had founded the Mercury Theatre, a
repertory company known for its high-quality experimental
productions. Houseman and Welles also produced the Mercury Theatre on the Air, a series of radio dramas which included a famous 1938 adaptation of the H. G. Wells novel
The War of the Worlds, about an invasion of the United
States by aliens. Directed and narrated by Welles, the program was so realistic that some listeners believed that an
army of Martians had actually landed in New Jersey.

Wright was thrilled at the prospect of working with
Houseman, who had exhibited sensitivity on racial issues
and a willingness to take artistic chances. Anyone willing to
adapt *Native Son* for the stage risked alienating white audiences who might be as terrified by the intimation of interracial sexual tension as they were by Mary Dalton's murder.
Wright was particularly excited at the prospect of working
with Welles, whose genius was already widely recognized,
though he had yet to produce his best-known work. When
Houseman approached Welles about directing *Native Son*,
he was shooting his masterpiece film *Citizen Kane*, but to
Wright's delight he agreed to make directing the adaptation
of the novel his next project.

Houseman was a strong believer in Wright's talent, and
he wanted to be sure that the character of Bigger Thomas
could be accurately translated to the stage. He hoped that
Wright could write the script himself, telling him, "The
more of your help we can have, the more you can transmit
to us of the intention and spirit of your book, the better
pleased we shall be." Although Wright had flirted with the
idea of writing for the theater during his time in Chicago,

he was not confident that he knew enough about the discipline of scriptwriting to accomplish this task by himself. He wanted the script to be worthy of the talents of Houseman and Welles, and he thought it wise to find a collaborator, someone whose knowledge of the theater was far greater than his own.

He settled upon Paul Green, a white North Carolinian who had become well known for his depictions of African-American life in the South. Green's 1926 play *In Abraham's Bosom* had been awarded a Pulitzer Prize for its moving story of the trials of a Southerner of mixed racial ancestry who opens a school as part of an effort to uplift other African Americans. Above all, Wright wanted to make sure that Bigger's humanity would come across in the stage production, and he admired Green's skill in creating believable black characters. The two agreed to collaborate on the project. Green would bring his skills as a playwright; and Wright would provide not only the intellectual property of the story but also his knowledge of the black, urban experience.

From the very beginning Houseman was leery of this collaboration. He worried that Green's fundamentally religious orientation would clash with Wright's atheistic outlook and that Green's rural Southern sensibilities would clash with the gritty urban setting of *Native Son*. He was also concerned—rightfully as it turned out—about the dynamics that might develop between the older, Pulitzer Prize–winning white man and the younger, less established black writer. Unusually sensitive about the issue of Southern racism, Green endeavored to treat Wright with social equality. Houseman recalled that when Wright visited Green to discuss the possibility of working together, "he could not have been more courteous, thoughtful and hospitable" to his African-American guest. But his egalitarianism was also plagued by limitations. Years later, after Wright's death, when reflecting upon their collaboration, Green sheepishly recalled that Wright had addressed him as "Mr. Green" while he had referred to Wright as "Richard." In artistic matters, Green proved to be even less sensitive, expecting the creator of *Native Son* to concede to his artistic vision.

For five weeks the two men worked together in Chapel Hill where Green lived while teaching at the University of North Carolina. Both the school and the town were intensely segregated, but Green received special permission to work with Wright in an office on campus, which was nearly deserted during the hot summer of their collaboration. Because he could not stay in the segregated campus guest facilities, Green found Wright lodging in a nearby black neighborhood. Even with these precautions, Wright's presence became known, and local residents who resented his work with Green and his secretary on equal terms threatened to harm him if he did not leave town. As harrowing as it must have been for Wright to sample once again the limits of Southern racial tolerance, it was in many ways one of the least surprising aspects of his uneasy partnership with Green.

Despite agreeing to adapt the novel for the stage, Green proved to be largely unsympathetic to Wright's vision. He did not wish to portray Bigger as someone who was purely a product of his environment, wanting instead to give him some personal responsibility for his fate. He also wanted a more sympathetic, more spiritual Bigger, a figure much different from the character Wright had already emblazoned on the literary landscape. Green also interjected the play with spirituals and a dream sequence, devices that ultimately muted the realism of the novel. In the process of creation, Green seemed to forget that Bigger Thomas was Wright's invention, and he repeatedly proved unwilling to compromise with the younger writer.

Houseman and Welles were appalled at Green's distortion of the original text and refused to produce the play as written. Instead they enlisted Wright to rewrite the script himself, adhering closely to the original mood of the novel. Green could not force Houseman and Welles to produce the play as he had written it, but he refused to change the official version of the script which was already under contract to be published by Harper & Brothers. Ultimately the play that was produced differed significantly from the play as published. Green dissociated himself from the theatrical production; Houseman and Welles refused to allow their names to be used on the dust jacket of the published version.

After this bizarre compromise of sorts, the men set about casting the play. The former boxer and talented actor Canada Lee was chosen to play the lead. Wright was thrilled by this choice, and the critics ultimately agreed that Lee was remarkably adept at capturing the anger and fear of Bigger as Wright had imagined him. The first white woman cast to play Mary Dalton withdrew after pressure from family and friends convinced her that the controversial play might damage her career. Twenty-two-year-old Anne Burr was selected to be her replacement, and she performed the role to Welles's satisfaction. Ever the perfectionist, Welles scrutinized every facet of the final production, refusing to open the show until every detail was to his liking. He delayed opening night twice, once because he thought the technicians were too clumsy and slow making scene changes. The play finally opened on March 25, 1941.

Despite the fact that it dealt with controversial subject matter and had a biracial cast, a rarity at the time, the play received mostly favorable reviews. The *New York Times* declared it "the biggest American drama of the season." It ran for 15 weeks on Broadway with 115 performances. Although initial interest was considerable, attendance soon fell off. The novelty faded, and some negative reviews encouraged theatergoers to stay away. Writing in the pages of the *Nation*, Joseph Wood Crutch gave what he admitted was a "minority report" on the quality of the production, which he described as "noisy" and "dull." Ultimately the play, which was Houseman and Welles's final collaboration, lost the company $36,000. A simplified traveling version of *Native Son* toured that summer, playing to packed audiences, particularly in black neighborhoods. Despite the number of artistic names involved in the theatrical version of *Native Son*, the play generated but a fraction of either the controversy or the praise that had greeted the novel.

Wright had his difficulties with Paul Green, but he enjoyed collaborating with Houseman and Welles and was thrilled to see Bigger brought to life so skillfully by Canada Lee. He liked seeing his work performed on the big stage. Opportunity for another chance to merge his writing with the world of performance came a few months after the opening of *Native Son*, when the well-respected critic and music producer John Hammond suggested that Wright try his hand at writing blues lyrics. Long a fan of the boxer Joe Louis, Wright thought Louis might be a compelling subject for his debut as a songwriter. One of Wright's first published pieces had been an article about Louis's victory over Max Baer, "Joe Louis Uncovers Dynamite," which appeared in *New Masses* in 1935. He had rejoiced again in print over Louis's highly symbolic triumph over the German boxer Max Schmeling in an article entitled "How He Did It—and Oh!—Where Were Hitler's Pagan Gods?" which appeared June 22, 1938, in the *Daily Worker*. Now he would celebrate Louis again in song.

Wright identified with Louis's journey from Southern poverty to international fame and saw him as a larger-than-life hero, a living and breathing refutation of both American and Nazi beliefs about black racial inferiority. In his

thirteen-stanza blues, "King Joe," Wright invokes the language of African-American folktales to describe Louis as
a man more powerful than a machine. Count Basie set
Wright's lyrics to music, and Paul Robeson performed "King
Joe" in his first-ever blues performance. John Hammond recorded the session, and the record of this dream-team collaboration of African-American artists sold forty thousand
advance copies.

No longer a somewhat obscure writer known only in leftist circles, Wright was frequently startled anew to discover
how widespread his appeal had become. He was stunned in
1941 when the National Association for the Advancement of
Colored People announced that he was to be given the prestigious Spingarn Medal in June at their thirty-second annual
meeting in Houston. The Spingarn Medal is still awarded
annually to African Americans who have excelled in their
field of endeavor. Wright, of course, was chosen on the basis
of the critical successes of *Uncle Tom's Children* and *Native
Son*, books that the NAACP described as "powerful" in their
ability to capture the "proscription, segregation, and denial
of opportunities to the American Negro." As a Communist,
Wright would have once regarded the NAACP as a moderate,
bourgeois organization, but he was undeniably flattered by
its recognition. After learning that he would receive the
award, he effused to his friend Claude Barnett, the founder
of the Associated Negro Press, "Honestly, I am beginning to
feel almost *respectable!*"

The Spingarn Medal award ceremony turned out to be a
bittersweet occasion. Although he was honored to receive
the award, the event led to yet another confrontation with
the leadership of the Communist party, souring Wright once
again on his involvement with the organization. He was infuriated when he was ordered by the party not to give his
planned speech at the award ceremony. He must have been

Wright receives the NAACP's Spingarn Award from Elmer Carter, editor of the National Urban League's *Opportunity* magazine, in 1941. *(Library of Congress)*

reminded of his ninth-grade valedictorian address, when he had sparred with the principal who refused to let him compose his own speech. As a child, Wright had refused to recite the speech the principal had written, insisting upon speaking his own words and trying to convey his own deepest thoughts. In this instance, however, he bowed to the demands of the party and chose not to give an address that discouraged African Americans from supporting U.S. involvement in the coming world war.

His remarks, instead of the more polemical speech he had planned, were nonetheless deeply moving. Directing the limelight off of himself and his own achievements, Wright eloquently accepted the award "in the name of the stalwart, enduring millions of Negroes whose fate and destiny I have sought to depict." He also demonstrated that even at this moment of personal triumph, when it appeared he had over-come nearly every limitation of his past, his memories of childhood and his sense of connectedness to his roots had not faded. Not wishing to exclude himself from the larger narrative of African-American history, he personalized his connection to the black freedom struggle, proclaiming, "I accept this award in the name of my father, a sharecropper on a Mississippi plantation and in the name of my mother who sacrificed her health on numerous underpaid jobs."

With its eloquence and humility, his speech hit just the right emotional note. Although some members of the black community had been uncomfortable with his depiction of black life in *Native Son*, thus finding him unworthy of the Spingarn Medal, their objections were weak and muted. De-spite the acclaim for his appearance, Wright seethed over the party's role in shaping his remarks that evening. For years he had resented the various claims the party had made on his time and the way party leaders continued to infringe on his intellectual and artistic independence. As he accepted the Spingarn Medal, he was about to reach his breaking point.

In addition to his personal resentments, Wright and many other American Communists found themselves frus-trated by abrupt shifts in party policy, which were precipi-tated by international events rather than by local concerns. As fascism began to rise in Europe and Asia in the 1930s, the Comintern, the international association of Commu-nist parties, ordered a shift in international policy. Instead of emphasizing its revolutionary agenda, the party was now willing to cooperate with any group that opposed fascism. In the United States this meant widespread party support for

Franklin D. Roosevelt's New Deal and for the activities of labor unions. It also meant a greater willingness to cooperate with mainstream civil rights organizations, such as the NAACP, in the fight against racism. For a time communism seemed to be edging toward the mainstream. But party priorities shifted abruptly again in 1939 when, unexpectedly, Stalin signed a nonaggression pact with Hitler. Now international Communists could no longer view fascism as an enemy. They were forced to abandon the Popular Front coalitions they had carefully built as their crusade against fascism turned into a crusade for peace.

Although these sharp twists and turns of policy were bewildering to many, Wright's faith was not shaken. He too was against U.S. involvement in a European conflict against fascism. He saw the war as irrelevant to him, as a senseless struggle among power-hungry capitalist nations. American racism, he argued, ought to be addressed before America committed itself to fighting a war in Europe. He first published his objections to African-American involvement in the growing conflict as "Not My People's War" in the June 17, 1941, issue of *New Masses.*

When Wright's essay appeared, his personal point of view was in complete alignment with official Comintern policy. But this abruptly changed when Hitler violated his pact with Stalin and invaded the Soviet Union on June 22, 1941, just days after Wright's article appeared. Immediately party policy shifted, and the Communists became strong supporters once again of the struggle against fascism. Wright was caught in the crossfire when he was suddenly forbidden to speak out against the war at the Spingarn ceremony. He resented being asked to change his opinion almost overnight in response to events overseas rather than to a quiet evolution in his own analysis of the situation.

Wright was not intransigent and was willing to change his mind as circumstances changed. He too eventually supported U.S entry in World War II after the bombing of Pearl Harbor on December 7, 1941, even allowing his name to be used to promote the sale of war bonds. In his mind, though, the issue of racism at home was linked with the war. He became one of the many supporters of the "Double V" campaign promoted by the *Pittsburgh Courier*. Black Americans should fight for victory against fascism in Europe and Asia as well as for victory against racism at home. But for the Communist party, victory against fascism was the primary goal. The struggle against racism could wait; indeed it should wait if it proved to be a distraction in the fight against Hitler.

Wright was particularly infuriated when the Communists announced they would oppose labor leader A. Philip Randolph's proposed demonstration against segregation in the military and discrimination in defense industry jobs. Although Wright wanted an American victory in the conflict, he was ambivalent about the role African Americans should be asked to play in securing that victory. Blacks, he believed, should not be expected to serve in a Jim Crow army, where even the blood they donated was placed in segregated blood banks. For the Communists, the issue of American racism was, for the time being, secondary. Wright could not accept this position, and quietly he decided to leave the party. He did not make a public declaration of his decision at the time, but in his mind his choice was irreversible.

Because of his involvement with the Communist party, Wright had been under FBI surveillance since at least the late 1930s. The agency's interest in him increased with the 1941 publication of *12 Million Black Voices*, a book some agents saw as seditious. Ironically, given FBI chief J. Edgar Hoover's ongoing obsession with communism, it was not until 1944, after Wright had broken his ties with the party, that the bureau added him to their "Security Index." This list contained the names of individuals considered such a threat to national security that the FBI was prepared, in the event of an emergency, to round them up and incarcerate them without due process. Leaving the party thus did little to diminish the intelligence community's interest in Wright, who remained under surveillance for the rest of his life. He expressed his annoyance at being watched in an unpublished 1949 poem, "The FB Eye Blues," where he complained, "Each time I love my baby, government knows it all."

Wright had good reason to be leery of the attention of the federal government, and during the war his anxieties were further heighted by the possibility of being drafted. He was chilled when he received a letter from the Brooklyn draft board in July 1942 telling him to report within ten days for a physical examination. As a married man with a young daughter, he had not expected to be drafted. Had he been classified 1-A because of his race or his notoriety? Determined not to serve in the Jim Crow armed forces, Wright immediately began asking influential friends and acquaintances for help. He was willing to support the war effort but not at the price of his own personal dignity. If the military could offer him a writing commission, he would accept it, but he would not serve as a soldier in a segregated unit, even if he had to flee to Canada or Mexico to avoid the draft. Although his friends sprang into action on his behalf, going so far as to contact Eleanor Roosevelt, he was not offered a position as a writer. But whether by serendipity or through his friends' connections, in October he received a letter saying he had been reclassified 3-A. Because he was thirty-three years old and had three dependents (his wife, his daughter, and his mother to whom he still sent money in Chicago), he would not be called to serve. His friends Ralph Ellison and

St. Clair Drake were not as fortunate as Wright, who was to spend the war years in Brooklyn writing. Like Wright, Ellison and Drake were adamant that they would not serve in a segregated army. Instead they chose to enlist in the integrated U.S. Merchant Marine, delivering supplies and troops to support the combat effort.

Freed from fretting about the draft and liberated from the anxiety of holding up his creative work to the scrutiny of the Communist party, Wright was able to spend the remainder of 1942 concentrating in earnest on his writing. Since shortly after he completed *Native Son* he had been working intermittently on a novel he was referring to as "Black Hope." Although never published, Wright attended to it over the course of six years. It is unique in the corpus of his writing because it is the only time he attempted to write from the point of view of a female protagonist. Maude Hampton, the central character in the book, is a light-skinned black woman who makes a decision to pass for white. In the process she earns the affection of a white millionaire and becomes financially comfortable. But she is plagued by guilt for her decision to deny her racial background, and ultimately she commits suicide.

The fact that Wright worked so diligently on this uncompleted manuscript is more than an interesting side note, because in the years since his death many feminist critics have disdained his portrayal of women in his fiction. His female characters, many argue, are stereotyped and one-dimensional. Some are portrayed as simpleminded and devoutly religious. Others are described primarily as sexual objects. At least in this instance, Wright endeavored to create a fictional world from a richly imagined female point of view.

Wright's life experiences may offer clues to why his creative powers often seemed to fail him when it came to creating female characters. His relationship with his mother and with the other women in his family had been tense because he could not embrace their religious worldview, and they resented his skepticism. Granny and Aunt Addie interpreted Wright's religious doubts as a rejection not just of faith but also of his family. Despite this family turmoil, he loved his mother and was close to some of his other female relatives, particularly his Aunt Maggie. One of his first purchases from his royalties for *Native Son* was a house in Chicago where his mother could live. But his sense of duty and affection was always clouded by a lingering resentment toward the rigid religious dogma that had governed Granny's home when he was a child.

Wright had had many female lovers, black and white, rich and poor, self-consciously intellectual and unabashedly frivolous. Although he was always searching for more satisfying female relationships than those he had known as a child, he may also have been repeating familiar patterns of behavior. He remained scarred by the lingering chill of Granny's self-righteousness, and he brought the suspicions and ideas about gender differences that he had formed during his childhood into each new relationship. He had difficulty making deep emotional connections. He left relationships abruptly, fleeing when faced with emotions he did not know how to cope with.

Even in his relationship with Ellen, by far his most successful romantic connection, he had difficulty sustaining emotional intimacy, often indulging in extramarital liaisons and retreating frequently into the private world of his thoughts. The most detailed description of a romantic relationship in Wright's fiction is in *The Outsider* (1953). The African-American protagonist in the novel, Cross Damon, falls in love with a lovely white Communist, Eva Blount. Although that fictional relationship, like most of Wright's real ones, was destined to fail, Wright's fictional creations

longed to save their doomed relationship, wanting to believe that a profound romantic connection could provide a
sense of meaning in an incomprehensible universe. Perhaps
Wright harbored the same secret hope.

It is tempting but dangerous to conflate a creative writer's
life with the fictional worlds he creates. Whether Cross and
Eva contained composite parts of Richard and Ellen is only
a matter of speculation. It is certain, however, that Wright
began to examine concretely the relationship between his
own life and his creative work beginning in 1943 when he
started toying with the idea of writing a literary autobiography. Since the publication of *Native Son*, Wright had written a brilliant photo-documentary entitled *12 Million Black
Voices*. Using poetic prose, he narrated the collective story
of the Great Migration, which was designed to accompany
photographs of black life in both the rural South and the
urban North taken by the talented WPA photographer Edwin
Rosskam. The effect of their combined efforts was so moving that Ralph Ellison recalled holding the book in his hands
and crying "over the painful pattern of remembered things."
Writing in the *Pittsburgh Courier*, Horace Cayton praised
the book for being "magnificent in its simplicity, directness,
and force." The blend of literary language with a story that
was factually true had a unique resonance for the readers of
12 Million Black Voices. While readers of *Native Son* could
and indeed did argue over the plausibility of Wright's charac-
terization of Bigger, a fictional character, they had difficulty
expressing that same degree of skepticism over real people
and documentable historical events.

In 1943 Wright and Cayton accepted the invitation of
Charles S. Johnson, head of sociology at Fisk University, to
come to Nashville and give talks on the historically black
campus. While there, Wright discovered once again how
powerful it could be to tell a story and label it "true." Earlier

he had been offered several invitations to visit Fisk, which he had turned down, perhaps because of his busy schedule. He may also have been reluctant to subject himself once again to the indignities of travel in the South. This time, however, Cayton waged a successful campaign to persuade Wright to accept the invitation. Wright acquiesced and flew to Chicago to join Cayton, and the two boarded a train for the South.

Their trip was uneventful. The two men had a private compartment on the train where they could relax, drink Scotch, and escape from any Jim Crow indignities they might encounter. Wright was fascinated by the Fisk campus, which had been founded six months after the end of the Civil War. The first students of the institution had been former slaves who were desperate for an education. This was a sentiment that Wright could certainly identify with. At times he had trouble connecting with college-educated blacks who had come from more privileged backgrounds than his. But he certainly felt no class resentment when he imagined what the Fisk Free Colored School must have symbolized to its first generation of students. By the time Wright arrived, the school had been transformed into a respectable institution of higher learning, which could boast the preeminent African-American activist and intellectual W. E. B. Du Bois among its alumni. Wright surely appreciated the fact that Du Bois was not the only former Fisk student to engage in social protest. In 1924 Fisk students had forced the white president of the institution to resign after he urged them to accept the constraints of the caste system. When Cayton and Wright arrived, the student body was black and most of the faculty was white. But more change was on its way. In 1947 their host, Charles Johnson, was to be named the institution's first African-American president.

Wright was to give his talk on April 9, 1943, in the lovely
Fisk Memorial Chapel, which had been erected in 1892.
He was an able and effective speaker but was sometimes
anxious about public speaking, preferring to express himself in writing. He struggled to find the right topic for this
talk. Not only was he appearing in such a storied historical
site, for the first time he was also speaking to an integrated
Southern audience. He finally decided to call his remarks
"What I've Been Thinking," and later described them as a
"clumsy, conversational kind of speech." He talked about
his Southern childhood and reflected on what it meant to be
a black man in the United States. As he spoke, he noticed
that the audience was "terribly still." They were stunned
by the frank, vivid way he described American racism and
moved by the episodes he so skillfully related from his own
life story. It was an intense experience for Wright. When he
saw the impact his words were having on the audience, he
was eager to get away. It was exhausting for him to reveal
so much of himself to a room filled with strangers. Later he
confessed that telling the truth about himself was "the hard-
est thing on earth"—but also worthwhile. After his talk, a
man rushed up to Wright and applauded him for being "the
first man to speak the truth in this town!"

After that experience, Wright decided to put his novel
aside temporarily and begin work on an autobiography. Although it would be painful to relive his childhood experiences, and he would be making himself vulnerable by reveal-
ing so much of his inner self, the reaction of the audience at
Fisk convinced him that his life story could dramatize the
impact of racism in a fresh way. He produced a draft of the
book in fewer than eight months. Interestingly, he chose to
end the book during his years in Chicago. He did not include the publication of *Native Son* in his life story, and he
certainly did not allude to the fact that he had since become

famous. Perhaps he made that decision because these events were too close to him and resisted the detachment brought by a greater passage of time. But he may also have decided he wanted to emphasize that his life had been typical rather than exceptional.

Wright ran the risk that his indictment of racism would be diluted if he reported overcoming it too completely. He wanted his readers to know that many African Americans could tell similar stories about racism and deprivation—but of course most did not become best-selling writers. It might be testing the limitations of some of his readers to ask them to understand that he was a well-known writer but still a victim of racism. Americans, he once complained, "cannot understand a man being gloomy if he had a pile of money." His success may have softened the blow of American racism, but it could not completely blunt it. To ask his readers to understand his current predicament might have been asking too much.

In what must have sounded like false modesty, Wright told the *New York Post*, "One of the things that made me write is that I realize I am a very average Negro." He insisted on the representative nature of his experience in part because he was determined "to give, to lend my tongue to the voiceless Negro boys." In spite of his great accomplishments and his frequent sense of loneliness and isolation, he continued to feel deeply connected to his community of origin. After his autobiography appeared in print he wrote two somewhat sheepish letters to his childhood friend and faithful correspondent Joe C. Brown, asking questions about their mutual friends and promising in the future not to "let your kind letters to me gather dust." He felt guilty for allowing himself to lose touch with his roots, and in private he wondered if his furtive sense of his own distinctiveness was merely wishful thinking. He confessed to his diary, "when

I was younger I used to say I was different from everybody else because I knew I was like everybody else."

His decision to conjure up agonizing past memories and to grapple with his complicated sense of himself simultaneously as an individual answerable to no one and as a spokesperson for his community paid off. Paul Reynolds was enthusiastic about the manuscript, and, as he predicted, Edward Aswell leaped at the opportunity to publish the book. Once again the Book-of-the-Month Club expressed an interest in the manuscript too. As with *Native Son,* they would consider the book only if Wright agreed to make certain changes. This time the club was even more heavy-handed in its desire to exert editorial control over the final product. Dorothy Canfield Fisher and other members of the selection committee made it very clear that they were interested only in the first section of the manuscript, "Southern Night," which described Wright's earliest years and his journey out of the South. They did not care for the second part of the book, "The Horror and the Glory," about Wright's experiences in Chicago, specifically his involvement with the Communist party. They also did not like Wright's working title for the book: *American Hunger.*

Once again Wright acceded to the club's demands. For someone who prided himself on his unwillingness to compromise his own personal integrity, he made notable concessions to his literary vision in the publication of his two most acclaimed books. In purely financial terms he would have been foolish not to agree to the club's demands. With its endorsement, the book was guaranteed to be successful, and Wright had a family to support with his writing. Undoubtedly, however, this editorial streamlining altered the meaning of the text.

Many have argued that the first part of the autobiography is better written and that truncating the text elevated its stature as a work of art. Ed Aswell, for example, had reservations about the Chicago passages, which he thought formed the least finely crafted section of the manuscript. Whatever the artistic merits of these changes, there is no doubt they altered the political message of the book. Originally Wright continued his indictment of American racism in recounting his Chicago years, refuting the idea that racism was a uniquely Southern problem. The new story structure forced readers to fill in the blanks for themselves, to posit their own theories about his future. They could read his escape from the South as a variation of the Horatio Alger story, the tale of a young African-American boy who through tenacity and intelligence managed to overcome the limitations of his backward Southern youth and escape to the more enlightened North. It had not been Wright's intentions to let Chicago off that easily. Racism, in his analysis, was an American problem, not a Southern anomaly.

Not content only to alter the structure of the book, Fisher also asked Wright to infuse more optimism into the concluding pages of the shortened text. This was asking too much. Wright made some small changes, but he refused to placate her entirely, to embrace her sentimental belief in the power of American ideals to alter social realities. What he had already written, he informed her, was "emotionally right." In the end, she decided not to push Wright any further, and the Book-of-the-Month Club announced its decision to adopt the book. The only issue remaining was the title. One of the judges suggested calling the truncated text *First Chapter.* Wright objected, preferring *Southern Night,* which both the judges and Aswell rejected. Finally Wright proposed *Black Boy.* It was memorable and direct, and it furthered Wright's aim of using his individual voice to capture the experiences of a larger group of people.

When *Black Boy* appeared in March 1945, it quickly outsold even *Native Son*. In only a matter of months, book sales reached the half-million mark. Wright was flooded with enthusiastic fan mail, and most critics applauded his accomplishments. Lionel Trilling labeled it a "remarkably fine book." Some naysayers were less impressed. Although Du Bois had been a fan of Wright's effort to narrate a chapter of African-American history in *12 Million Black Voices*, he was far less enthusiastic about Wright's attempt to relate his own personal story. Du Bois found *Black Boy* to be "patently and terribly overdrawn." The narrator, he sneered, was a "brat." Even though Wright self-consciously set out to speak for other "black boys" as well as for himself, Du Bois was unconvinced, writing in the *New York Herald Tribune*, "The hero . . . is self-centered to the exclusion of everybody and everything else."

Once again, however, praise for Wright more or less drowned out the occasional criticisms. He was now in higher demand than ever before for interviews and speaking engagements, which he tolerated in order to promote the book and to enhance his bank account. He and Ellen needed the money to pay for their new home in Greenwich Village. And Wright had been toying with the idea of an extended stay outside the United States. Now that World War II was drawing to a close, he hoped at long last to travel to Europe. The more money he could accumulate, the more options he would have.

Although he detested much of the "noise" that his wildly successful book was generating and wished that he could "run away" from the ringing telephone, in the year between October 1945 and 1946 he agreed to give a total of forty-six lectures. He gamely set out on the tour, speaking at a several venues in the Northeast and in the Midwest. The grueling schedule was exhausting. He missed Ellen and Julia, and on the road he seemed more than usually prone to sickness. He decided to abandon the tour in midstream, apologetically admitting that this agenda "wears me too thin."

He was also growing weary of the racism that he and his family faced during their daily lives in New York. Unquestionably life in the North brought with it numerous advantages. His marriage to Ellen, after all, would have been illegal in Mississippi. Being seen in public with her, married or otherwise, could have meant a death sentence in the South. There was no question that he had greater freedom of association and action and more opportunities in the North than he ever could have hoped for had he not migrated. Still, the daily insults were tiring. He never knew which restaurants or hotels would admit him, or once admitted how he would be treated. He resented the hostile stares and the difficulties he had accomplishing even simple things like securing a mortgage to buy a home. As much as it bothered him when he was mistreated, he had an even harder time watching his family suffer. The three of them could not appear on the street together without being insulted or stared at.

His most painful experience was watching Julia learn about racism. He adored his little girl and longed to shield her. From the moment she was born she had caused a stir. Ellen had heard nurses at the hospital sputter about the "black" baby. Constance Webb, the white wife of C. L. R. James, remembered one tense moment she had when shopping with little Julia. The child told her that she needed to use the restroom, and Webb took her inside the Bergdorf Goodman department store on Fifth Avenue to use the toilet. Once inside, Julia was rebuffed by a salesperson who hissed, "There are no restrooms for *you!*" When Webb reported the incident to Wright, he was outraged.

To Wright the way to shield Julia seemed obvious. It was the same solution he had taken as a teenager when he decided to leave Mississippi. They would flee. He would seek out yet another place and hope that he could find a more tolerant atmosphere, a place where he and Ellen and Julia would be judged on their accomplishments, not on the racial composition of their family. Chicago and New York had been an improvement over Mississippi and Arkansas, but Wright was no longer content to accept the somewhat ameliorated racism of the urban North. Even if he could learn to tolerate the racist slights and therapeutically to deal with the indignities of racism in his writing, everything had changed now that he had a daughter. He was responsible for her well-being; there had to be another way of living, another environment where she could be free from the potentially crippling burden of American racism. He and his family would travel. They would experience another way of living; they would go to France and see if things were any different there.

CHAPTER SIX

Expatriate

୬୭ During the war years, when travel to Europe was impossible, the Wright family enjoyed two long vacations in Quebec, which Wright regarded as the closest he could then get to France. Richard and Ellen also began taking French lessons so that they could better enjoy their vacations in Canada and prepare themselves should the opportunity to travel to Europe arise. As soon as they began seriously to consider leaving the United States, France seemed to be the obvious place to go. In the 1920s the country had been a haven for the writers of the so-called Lost Generation, such as F. Scott Fitzgerald and Ernest Hemingway. The artistic freedom they had enjoyed there was greater than in the United States, where books were still regularly banned. Artists fleeing American Puritanism and materialism had created a lively expatriate community in Paris centered on Sylvia Beach's English-language bookshop Shakespeare & Company. Wright had come of age as a writer while hearing stories about the fabled Americans who had dared to leave their country behind and whose creative powers had seemingly flourished in their new environment.

In addition to its reputation as a haven for writers, Paris held a special place in the African-American imagination. Black writers of the Harlem Renaissance like Langston Hughes and Countee Cullen had enjoyed extended stays there, reveling not only in the thriving artistic community but also in the more racially tolerant atmosphere. Paris became a gathering place too for African-American jazz musicians who played to wildly appreciative crowds at many of the city's hotspots. The St. Louis–born black singer and dancer Josephine Baker, who performed daringly in the almost nude, was one of the most popular performers in Paris from the 1920s until her death in 1975. In general the French were less race conscious than Americans, a fact that many black veterans of World War I had been able to confirm for themselves after visiting the country during wartime. For black entertainers, writers, and artists of every variety, at least a short stay in France seemed to be almost a mandatory part of one's artistic training.

The advent of World War II and the Nazi occupation of France drove out the vast majority of American visitors and expatriates. A very few particularly devoted Francophiles, including Josephine Baker, rode out the occupation. Baker showed her devotion to her adopted country by working with the French resistance. The American writer Gertrude Stein and her lover Alice B. Toklas also stayed in France, managing to survive the occupation despite their Jewish backgrounds. During the war years, jazz—which the Nazis regarded as decadent—had been driven underground and could no longer be heard in Paris nightclubs. After the four-year Nazi rule, the magical, artistically free Paris that had attracted Hemingway no longer existed. But when Paris was liberated in 1944, the French began to reclaim their city and to revive the decaying arts scene. After victory was declared in Europe, adventurers from throughout the world once again began traveling there, eager to revive the bygone mood of the 1920s. Wright was determined to become part of the new generation of artists to discover Paris.

The United States he was willing to leave behind in the 1940s was undergoing a sweeping transformation. Mobilization for the war had broken the back of the Great Depression, and after the conflict ended there seemed to be no limit to American prosperity. The GI Bill provided low-interest mortgages to veterans who enthusiastically began buying houses in the suburbs that sprang up almost overnight around major U.S. cities. GI college scholarships allowed many men who ordinarily would not have had the means to attend college to enroll, providing them with the education they needed to advance themselves and their families into the swelling ranks of the middle class. Americans owned more cars than ever before. Department stores proudly displayed such labor-saving devices as modern washing machines, which more and more consumers could now afford. Glossy magazines advertised new and better convenience foods. Everywhere Wright looked, he saw Americans celebrating their newfound abundance and prosperity.

In contrast, France was in economic shambles when the war ended. Even basic necessities like food and coal were in short supply. Luxury items like automobiles were enjoyed by only the fortunate few. The decision to go to Paris meant that Wright would have to forgo some of the material comforts of living in the United States, at least in the short term. He liked to live well. His bohemian friends and former comrades had frequently been surprised, appalled, or amused upon visiting his New York apartment to discover elegant furniture and dishes, which had been carefully selected by Ellen. But material comfort alone could never satisfy Wright; he had survived with far less in the past.

Because Europe was unstable and in the midst of reconstruction, the U.S. State Department was cautious in issuing passports to Americans who wished to travel there.

Wright did everything in his power to present an airtight case for his need to travel to France. His friend Dorothy Norman agreed to let him represent her journal *Twice a Year* in Paris. A fluent French speaker and an admirer of French culture, Norman had already introduced Wright to a number of French intellectuals, including Jean-Paul Sartre and Albert Camus, at a gathering at her East Seventieth Street home. She was an enthusiastic champion of Wright's desire to go abroad, and she wrote to the State Department on his behalf. Gertrude Stein, one of the most famous American expatriates then residing in Paris, put in a good word for him with her friends at the American embassy in Paris. Other friends contacted famed anthropologist and French attaché Claude Lévi-Strauss, telling him about Wright's desire to visit France. In response, Lévi-Strauss astounded Wright by inviting him to go as an official guest of the French government. The struggling country even agreed to pay for Wright's passage to Europe and for a month's living expenses while he was there. With this strong support of friends on both sides of the Atlantic, the State Department agreed to issue passports for the entire family, which Wright flew to Washington, D.C., to pick up in person.

When the Wright family arrived in Paris in May 1946, they saw that the stories that they had heard about French deprivation were true. While Americans were erecting modern suburban homes, many Parisians were living in unheated flats or cheap hotel rooms with shared bathrooms equipped with squat toilets. Wright learned that many of the writers who worked in the famous Paris cafés did so in order to escape from their own cold and squalid rooms. The Café de Flore and Café Les Deux Magots, favorite spots of Sartre and Simone de Beauvoir, appealed to the celebrated couple in part because they were warmer than their unheated apartments. The Wrights' first Paris residence, the Trianon Palace

Hotel where Gertrude Stein had reserved rooms for them, struck the Americans as rather dreary, encouraging them too to pass much of their time at local cafés.

Wright was impressed immediately not only by the different standards of living in France but by the stunning beauty of Paris. Often drab living conditions were masked by the city's magnificent architecture. Wright was able to take his first extended look at the city after Gertrude Stein and an official from the American embassy picked up the family at the train station upon their arrival on May 10. The driver took an indirect route to their hotel, allowing them a grand view of the city along the way. Wright was overcome with emotion as he took in his new surroundings, and could not help but to gasp, "How absolutely beautiful!" The monuments, gardens, and gleaming River Seine struck him as overpowering in their splendor. Nothing in his travels in North America could have prepared Wright for Paris with its Gothic cathedrals, the baroque and rococo magnificence of its palaces and museums, and the whimsical art nouveau entrances to the Paris Metro. He must have marveled at the way these competing styles somehow blended organically, belying the fact that the city had evolved gradually and had not sprung up in its present incarnation overnight.

The best thing about the city, however, the thing that Wright had been looking for, was the lack of race consciousness he discovered. His initial impressions confirmed the stories of French egalitarianism brought home by the writers of the Harlem Renaissance and black veterans of World War I. He could enter any café without anxiety about how he would be received. He was amazed to watch a white and black couple stroll down a boulevard hand in hand unmolested, greeted only by the bland disinterest of their fellow citizens. For the first time in his life he felt some of the awful tension of racism leave him, and he spent hours exploring the city and enjoying a kind of colorless individuality.

The family's first weeks in Paris were a social whirlwind. Wright was feted at a party sponsored by the government at the sumptuously decorated Hôtel de Ville, wined and dined by publishers, and entertained in Gertrude Stein's celebrated salon at her apartment at 27, rue de Fleurus. When Wright entered Stein's home he must have been aware of the famous footsteps he followed in. Pablo Picasso and Ernest Hemingway had once been frequent guests. Wright was merely the latest in an impressive string of geniuses whose talent Stein had admired and attempted to promote. With her typical certitude, after reading *Black Boy* she had labeled Wright "the best American writer today." Wright too was an admirer of Stein's experimental, modernist prose. He was particularly fond of her story "Melanctha," which had a black protagonist.

Like many of the renowned visitors before him, Wright enjoyed viewing Stein's modern art collection, which included works by Picasso, Cézanne, and Gauguin among others. When the Wrights visited, Stein likely welcomed them using her customary routine. Generally she held court with the mostly male writers, intellectuals, and artists who found their way to rue de Fleurus while her romantic partner and secretary, Alice B. Toklas, entertained their wives or female companions. Neither Stein nor Toklas, however, was particularly fond of Ellen Wright. In a brutally frank letter to Carl Van Vechten, Stein described her as "rather awful." They also found the presence of a very active four-year-old Julia quite draining. Upon her arrival Julia immediately spotted two ornate antique children's chairs, which had been covered with Toklas's embroidery of a custom design done by Pablo Picasso. As Julia headed toward the chairs, Stein scolded her. They were not to be used by children anymore.

Although Stein did not warm up to the Wright women, she initially liked Richard upon meeting him. Their relationship soon became strained, though, when one of Stein's friends borrowed a considerable sum of money from Wright, which he then refused to repay. As it turned out, Wright and Stein had precious little time to try to repair this falling out. Fewer than three short months after they met, Stein died of stomach cancer. In many ways her passing symbolized the end of an era. She had become synonymous with the Left Bank arts scene before World War II, and she had played an important role in creating the romanticized version of Paris that Wright had come looking for. But the 1940s and 1950s were to be a much different era. Wright, though he did not know it then, was to become the symbolic center of a new community of African-American expatriate artists and writers.

At the time the Wright family had not yet contemplated leaving the United States permanently. Although they enjoyed their stay in France immensely, they approached the trip as a lengthy vacation, a temporary reprieve from American racism, not necessarily the trial attempt at relocation that it appeared to be in retrospect. After struggling to arrange the financing for their Charles Street home in Greenwich Village, the family had not yet had a chance to live there as they waited for tenants to vacate the building. When it was finally empty, Ellen was eager to begin executing her plans for renovation. In December, after more than seven months in France, the Wrights decided it was time for them to resume their lives in New York.

On the way back to the United States, the family spent three weeks in London, a city that failed to hold the same charm for them as Paris. While they were there, however, Wright was able to spend a great deal of time with George Padmore, whom he had met through his friend C. L. R.

James. Like Wright, Padmore was a former member of the Communist party. He had risen high in the party ranks, even living for a time in the Soviet Union where he had headed the Negro Bureau of the Communist International Labor Unions. In the 1930s he became frustrated with the party after its once strong stance against colonialism weakened. He left the party and moved to London, where he devoted himself full time to his dearest goal, that of freeing Africa from European colonialism.

Padmore had close ties not only with fellow Trinidadian C. L. R. James but with the noted Trinidadian historian and politician Eric Williams. He served as a key adviser to Kwame Nkrumah, who was to become the first prime minister of Ghana after the country achieved independence from Britain. After that visit, Wright and Padmore developed a warm personal relationship that was to last until Padmore's death in 1959. His English wife Dorothy soon became one of Wright's correspondents, dutifully keeping him appraised of developments in the Pan-African movement. Spending time with the Padmores was intellectually stimulating for Wright. More and more he was beginning to see racism in the United States within the larger framework of the exploitation and oppression of people of color throughout the globe.

After the variety of his experiences in Paris and his lengthy conversations in the kitchen of the Padmores' London flat, Wright was returning to New York with a much more sophisticated view of the world and an enlarged set of personal possibilities. With the enthusiastic reception of *Black Boy* he had money in the bank. The problem of earning a living was solved for several years to come. He now had the luxury of a superabundance of choices. He could live where he wanted and work on the projects that suited him. He no longer had to fret about mere survival but could concern himself with how to best nourish his soul.

When Wright returned to New York he was distressed by the noisiness of the city but impressed, almost in spite of himself, with the abundance of material goods. He gawked at street vendors nonchalantly displaying piles of colorful fruit, something he had not seen during the past eight months in hunger-haunted Europe. Yet despite the prosperity that greeted him, or perhaps partially because of it, he felt suddenly alienated by the culture. Even in New York, the intellectual hub of the United States, his fellow citizens struck him as crass and materialistic. He missed the meandering intellectual conversations he had enjoyed in French cafés. Most offensive of all to his changed sensibilities was the racial climate he rediscovered at home. He was no longer used to being sneered at as he walked down the street with Ellen. He had lost some of the thick exterior he had acquired during his Mississippi youth. He had let down his guard in Paris, and he was now newly sensitive to the barrage of tiny insults that greeted him every day. On several occasions he was close to a breaking point. One day while having coffee with Constance Webb, the waitress served them both coffee laden with salt, telling them to leave the restaurant if they didn't like it. In Paris he had been toasted by government officials and celebrities in the opulent city hall. Now he was being derided as "boy" by New York shopkeepers and peddlers. Soon neither he nor Ellen felt they could continue to endure these petty insults. Within six months of their return to New York, the family departed again for Paris, never again to reside in the United States.

The family's second departure was on July 30, 1947, on a ten-day crossing aboard the *SS America*. This time they were also accompanied by their black-and-white cat Knobby and a shiny new Oldsmobile sedan. Wright kept a journal during the voyage and for his first three months in Paris. Sitting in his cabin, he confided to his typewriter, "I hope to remain away from America this time as long as possible." On board ship he was appalled by the behavior of the American passengers, which he compared unfavorably to that of the Europeans: "Beside the people of the Continent, Americans appear like country apes." Quick to offer criticism when he felt it was merited, Wright could also be critical of the French, whom he found to be less efficient and hardworking than Americans. After living in fast-paced New York, he knew he would have to readjust to the more leisurely tempo of Paris, where many shopkeepers enjoyed lengthy lunch breaks and much of the city shut down in August as Parisians went on vacation. He began to feel the strain of his conflicting cultural expectations shortly after their arrival.

Before leaving New York the Wrights had made arrangements to live temporarily with a friend they had met on their last visit, Odette Lieutier, who owned a large house at 9, rue de Lille. Lieutier managed a bookstore that specialized in the performing arts. She was a fluent English speaker with a wide circle of friends and was free-spirited, perhaps too much so for the more conventional Wright family. She was fond of bringing boisterous guests home for drinks, and the Wrights began to suspect that she also used drugs. On top of that, Lieutier was lackadaisical about housekeeping and unconcerned when the hot water would not work or the oven stopped functioning. Living in her house soon become intolerable to the Wrights due to their American sensibilities about bathing and Wright's partiality for cooking and baking at home. They would have to find their own apartment and design their own cultural enclave where they could enjoy both the comforts of their New York life and the cultural ambiance of Paris.

Due to a housing shortage, finding a suitable apartment would not be an easy task. Wright left this and most other household chores to Ellen who, after much searching, found a place in a posh neighborhood near the Bois de Boulogne. For the time being they would have to leave their beloved Left Bank neighborhood. As they settled in, Wright often ran errands around the city in his Oldsmobile, which suddenly seemed enormous as it rumbled down the narrow Paris side streets. Gasoline was rationed for French residents, but Wright found suppliers who were more than willing to sell him gasoline for his American dollars. He felt conspicuous driving the car. When the French saw him coming, he noticed that their "eyes bugged and their tongues clicked." He was not used to having a material advantage over anyone, and he was embarrassed by his relative wealth. Even though he was fleeing the country as a refugee from racism, Wright could not help but observe the peculiar way in which being an American worked to his advantage. He and Ellen had brought trunks of food from the United States, and unlike their French neighbors they were eligible to shop at the military-run American post exchange where they could use American dollars to buy goods unavailable elsewhere.

Their first weeks in Paris were busy. They had to navigate their way through the French bureaucracy to renew their identity cards. Wright kept having car trouble and found that French mechanics had difficulty fixing his large American car. After much searching, he found an American mechanic who could repair it. Knobby the cat ate some chicken bones and had to be taken on an emergency trip to the vet. After they moved into their new apartment they had to buy furniture and bookshelves. Their social calendar was more crammed than ever. They had to rekindle friendships they had begun during their first visit to Paris and to establish new connections. Moreover an unending stream of American acquaintances seemed to pass through the city, and they felt compelled to entertain them all. As a result,

Wright was restless, consumed with minutiae, and unable to concentrate on his writing.

During these early days of his return to Paris, he confided in his journal about his loneliness. He despaired that his "deepest thoughts [were] communicated to no one." The sense of isolation and separation from other people that had haunted him in Mississippi plagued him still. His entire life had been spent seeking out different geographies and experiences in the hope that he could find contentment. Everywhere he went he asked himself, "How can I live . . . freely?" "That," he declared, "is the question of my life." Much of his energy had been spent trying to escape from the indignities of racism, and he had been successful in gradually finding more and more open-minded people to befriend and increasingly tolerant cities to reside in. Now in Paris he had found a greater degree of social acceptance than he had ever enjoyed before, but he was still plagued by anxiety and discontent. He was now discovering that not all the demons he was fighting were external. He could change his environment, but he could not tame the internal regions of his own soul. His friend Edith Anderson observed, "Dick was looking for a home which did not exist for him on the planet." He had fled from Mississippi and New York, but he could never get away from himself.

In spite of Wright's melancholy, he endeavored to be dutiful, to fulfill his self-appointed mission as spokesperson for the oppressed. He also tried to be a good husband and father. In August 1947 he watched Ellen and Julia row a boat on a pond in the Bois de Boulogne. Never a fan of physical exertion, Wright elected not to join them, but as he watched from the shore he felt ashamed, as if he had failed them by not being the kind of husband and father they deserved. He hoped that somehow they could find a way to love him in spite of his inadequacies and to see him as he

Richard and Ellen Wright in 1950. By this time the happiest years of the Wrights' marriage were over, their relationship weakened by a series of extramarital affairs. *(Yale Collection of American Literature, Beinecke Rare Book and Manuscript Library)*

was, "a nervous, scared but somehow brave man who tries his goddamnest to do his best." Seeing his beloved wife and child gliding across the picturesque little lake, he could not have known it, but in many ways the happiest days of his life were already over. His writing would never again enjoy the critical acclaim and commercial success it had while he lived in the United States. His once-happy marriage to Ellen would soon begin to deteriorate as Wright tried to soothe his aching loneliness with a serious of extramarital affairs.

For the first five years in Paris, Wright published very little and was unable to produce another book. Michel Fabre, who wrote a well-regarded literary biography of Wright in 1973, refers to this time as Wright's "existentialist period," a label that he admits does not fully cover the scope of Wright's soul-searching. It does, however, come close. Although Wright was unable to make progress on a new novel he had begun before leaving the United States, he took advantage of his writer's block to begin a process of reeducation. While still living in New York he had become interested in the existentialist ideas circulating in Paris intellectual circles in the 1940s. He was acquainted with Jean-Paul Sartre, the thinker most identified with French existentialism, and he and Ellen were on particularly friendly terms with Sartre's companion, the writer and philosopher Simone de Beauvoir. Their friendship with her was so warm that she dedicated her 1948 book, *America Day by Day*, to Ellen and Richard Wright. The influence of de Beauvoir and other French intellectuals on Wright was profound. He made a point of reading the key texts of the existentialist movement. Three months after arriving in Paris, he read Albert Camus' *The Stranger* in English, slowly and carefully weighing every phrase. He sought to master not only the works of his contemporaries but also the precursors to modern existentialism, particularly Søren Kierkegaard's 1882 masterpiece *The Concept of Dread*.

Existentialism, with its emphasis on the primacy of one's subjective experience, appealed to Wright. By instinct he was an existentialist long before the term was coined. Sartre believed that "existence precedes essence," that the individual creates oneself through the process of making conscious, deliberate choices. Because individuals have no fixed essence, they are free to perpetually reinvent themselves, just as Wright had been doing since childhood. In *Black Boy* he proclaimed his lifelong conviction "that the meaning of living came only when one was struggling to wring a meaning out of meaningless suffering." Thus the high-toned intellectual discourse of existentialism that he discovered in Paris reinforced and refined his innate sense of how he should live. Like the French existentialists, Wright had long realized that the universe was absurd and that it was up to him to make sense of the senselessness. He found added intellectual kinship with Sartre and de Beauvoir with his belief that the freedom to choose was accompanied by tremendous responsibility, and that it was up to the committed writer to use his or her work to bring about political change for the better.

During his so-called existentialist period, his new outlook also influenced his aesthetic sensibilities. He was infected with the existentialist infatuation for the novel of ideas, when fiction is used to illustrate philosophical concepts. His next published novel, *The Outsider*, which appeared eight long years after *Black Boy* in 1953, reflects this reeducation. In this book Wright shed the social realism of his past work, which had made him so successful. In *The Outsider* he did not attempt to describe vividly a particular social reality. Instead he used the vehicle of the novel to grapple with the philosophical issues that consumed him. Although the protagonist of the book, Cross Damon, is an African American, Wright does not limit the scope of his analysis to the problem of American racism. He comments on "the problem and meaning of western civilization as a whole and the relation of Negroes and other minority groups to it." The protagonist is caught up in an absurd and meaningless existence until, somewhat like his literary predecessor Bigger Thomas, he looks for meaning by committing a series of murders. In one particularly brutal scene he kills both a Communist and a fascist, violently annihilating both alternative means of making sense of the universe. Damon is never able to extract any purpose or meaning from his existential freedom. At the end of the novel, on the verge of death, Damon sums up his motivation for living: "I wanted to be free . . . to feel what I was worth . . . what living meant to me . . ." When asked what he has found out in the course of his life, he answers, "Nothing."

The Outsider contains numerous ponderous passages undergirded by a thin plot, and left critics generally unenthusiastic. Nelson Algren, writing in the *Paris Review*, observed, "He's trying to write as an intellectual, which he isn't basically." De Beauvoir, Algren's secret paramour, privately agreed, labeling the book a "meaningless, crazy story." In the pages of *The Freeman*, Max Eastman remarked that Wright seemed to be "wrestling more earnestly with problems torturing his own mind in passing from the Communist conspiracy to the Existentialist racket than with those confronting his hero." Much to Wright's dismay, his attempts to be self-consciously intellectual and to envelop in one novel all he had learned since leaving the United States fell flat. Some of his acquaintances murmured that in leaving behind American racism, he had also left behind the concrete source of both his anger and his artistic strength.

While Wright was grappling with existentialism, he was also strengthening his commitment to Pan-Africanism. His travels had given him a broader view of the world, and his long conversations with George Padmore had bolstered his sense that racism in America was related to a series of struggles throughout the globe for the freedom of oppressed peoples. Due in large part to Padmore's influence, Wright became more and more interested in the intertwined experiences of the peoples of the African Diaspora. In Paris he got to know many individuals of African descent who came from French Africa and the French-speaking Caribbean. In 1947 he helped Léopold Senghor, Aimé Césaire, and Ailioune Diop, the leading members of the Négritude literary movement, found their landmark journal *Présence Africaine*. The first issue included the French translation of Wright's story "Bright and Morning Star."

The journal and the movement that produced it were designed to promote the shared heritage of people of African descent throughout the world and to agitate for liberation from colonialism. Although Wright felt a certain kinship with this group of black intellectuals, he found some aspects of Pan-Africanism unsettling. He was wary of the idea of racial essentialism that imprinted some of the writing associated with the movement. As an existentialist who believed that it was up to the individual to create his or her own essence, he resisted the idea of innate racial traits. He did not believe that he should be expected to feel an automatic kinship with anyone because of their shared African descent, regardless of their divergent interests or backgrounds. He preferred to judge people as individuals and wished to be viewed that way himself. Nonetheless he was completely dedicated to the Négritude movement's critique of colonialism. He was beginning to see that France was not the racial utopia he had imagined it to be and that the country had much to answer for in the way it treated its colonized subjects both abroad and at home.

Wright did not spend all his time in Paris reading philosophy or speaking out against colonialism. He enjoyed roaming the streets, having conversations in his favorite cafés, and dining at his growing number of prized restaurants. In her letters to Nelson Algren, Simone de Beauvoir refers fleetingly to a number of pleasant evenings spent with the Wrights. She enjoyed strolling through Paris with Wright because his enthusiasm for the city was so infectious. He was a gracious host to acquaintances who passed through the city, going out of his way to show them the sights through his eyes. In September 1947 one such visitor was Edith Anderson Schroeder.

Schroeder, who was white, was an attractive thirty-one-year-old Communist from New York who was staying in

Paris while waiting for permission to travel to Berlin to visit her German Communist husband. She had been encouraged to call Wright by her friend, the poet Naomi Replansky, who had been Wright's friend and sometimes lover in New York. As a dedicated Communist, Schroeder felt treasonous calling him. His quiet break from the party in 1942 had exploded into a public renunciation in 1944 when an exposé of his experiences with the party in Chicago, "I Tried to Be a Communist," appeared in the *Atlantic Monthly*. Schroeder's loneliness, however, overcame her political scruples. One weekend, while Ellen and Julia were away in the country, Schroeder and her friend Helen Weinstein visited Wright. She was amazed at the posh surroundings of the Wright apartment. She thought the living room resembled a hotel lobby and wrongly assumed that the furnishings Ellen had selected "were let with the apartment, for they gave no clue to personal idiosyncrasies."

Wright and Schroeder shared a short but intense friendship. They spoke of politics and literature, and Wright soon fell in love, telling her "what you evoke in me is something I've not yet felt for any other woman." Although he lured her into bed once, Schroeder generally rebuffed Wright's advances. She refused to take a trip with him to Monte Carlo, formally explaining, "The implications of such a trip are too foreign to my chief desires." Although she was flattered by the attention of the great man and treasured the letters he wrote to her after he left for Monaco alone to convalesce after a particularly bad bout of the flu, she was not physically attracted to him. Startled, Wright asked if she was refusing him because of his "color." He was not used to having his advances rejected.

Ellen likely noticed her husband's infatuation, making her disapproval known the only time Schroeder dined with the Wrights together. Ellen treated her coolly, neglecting to pass the butter or refill her plate. Schroeder, who had very little money to see her through her stay in Paris, smarted at this inhospitality from her well-fed host. After dinner, Ellen neither joined in the conversation nor left the room to allow the pair to converse in private. Schroeder knew this would be her last visit to the Wright apartment. Wright had had numerous casual affairs throughout the years of their marriage, which Ellen may or may not have known about. But Wright's affection for this "Funny-Faced" girl, as he called her, was particularly intense. In watching her husband swoon in Schroeder's presence, Ellen may have sensed that she was beginning to lose the closeness she and Wright had always shared.

For the time being, Schroeder traveled to Germany and the Wrights went about finding a permanent place to live in Paris. They enjoyed their attractive apartment at avenue de Neuilly, but both longed for the more bohemian atmosphere of the Left Bank. After much searching, in May 1948 they signed a long-term lease for an apartment at 14, rue Monsieur le Prince, only a short walk from the breathtaking Luxembourg Gardens. Now that they had found their ideal home, they were determined to make it comfortable. They added central heating to the apartment, a rare luxury in Paris. Ellen traveled to New York to sort through their items still in storage and to ship favorite possessions to Paris. They filled the apartment with paintings, copies of Wright's books, and furniture that was both elegant and comfortable. Their friend, the African-American writer Chester Himes, recalled that he "never ceased to regard Dick's apartment with envy and amazement." It certainly provided a stark contrast to the series of shabby hotel rooms where Himes lived. Wright's comfortable surroundings set him apart. He had become literary royalty on the Left Bank.

Now settled, Wright looked for a favorite neighborhood café. During his first visit to Paris he had followed in Sartre and de Beauvoir's footsteps at the Café de Flore or in Hemingway's at Café Les Deux Magots. Now he was no longer a tourist; it was time to seek out a place of his own. He and Ellen settled on the Café Monaco, just down the street from them at the intersection of the lively Boulevard St. Germain. They took their quest seriously. In trying to convey the importance of the French café scene to outsiders, Wright explained, "The determination of a café in which to spend one's hours of relaxation is a delicate problem, a matter of trial and error, tasting, testing the nature and quality of the café's atmosphere." The Monaco was a little shabby, and it certainly lacked the pretense and bustle of the better-known gathering spots. Inside, working-class Parisians mingled with French intellectuals and an eclectic international clientele, including many American GIs. Wright soon became a fixture at the Monaco, treated with deference by the owner who surely wished to encourage the patronage of the literary tourists and black expatriates who gathered there to bask in Wright's presence. Chester Himes recalled that once inside, Wright "greeted everyone with boisterous condescension; it was obvious he was the king thereabouts." He sometimes also went to the nearby Café de Tournon, another favorite spot for African-American expatriates who conversed against a backdrop of gaudy murals depicting the Luxembourg Gardens.

The Wright family's attachment to Paris grew stronger on June 17, 1949, when Ellen gave birth to another daughter, Rachel, the only member of the family to be born on foreign soil. Their youngest daughter was to have a very different upbringing from that of her older sister. When she learned to speak, Rachel insisted on conversing in French, a development that Wright should have been able to anticipate but

Wright outside a bookstore on the rue de Seine in the late 1950s, after his expatriation to Paris. *(Yale Collection of American Literature, Beinecke Rare Book and Manuscript Library)*

one that nonetheless struck a deep blow. He never mastered the French language himself. He could carry on halting conversations, but he could express himself freely only in his native tongue. This language barrier of sorts helped create an emotional distance between Rachel and her father. His ability to effectively bond with the little girl he described as "as pretty as a doll" was also hindered by his hectic travel schedule. Although he had been an actively involved coparent during the first few years of Julia's life, he spent a great deal of time away from Rachel, ceding to Ellen most of the responsibility for raising her. Just after Rachel's birth, he was in Rome for two weeks to promote an Italian translation of *Black Boy*. Soon after, he spent almost a year away from his family shooting a cinematic version of *Native Son*.

In the near decade since the publication of *Native Son*, Wright had been contacted by a number of people expressing interest in adapting the book for the screen. So far he had found no one who he was willing to entrust with his story; they all wanted changes that would radically alter the original plot or characters. One Hollywood producer, much to Wright's horror, had even proposed a movie with an all-white cast. In 1949, when French director Pierre Chenal approached Wright about making a film, the author was taken off guard. Although he was an enormous fan of the cinema and had long dreamed of seeing his work translated into a movie, he had all but given up on the likelihood of finding the right person to produce *Native Son*. After meeting Chenal, however, Wright was convinced that the director would respect his vision, and he agreed to the project. Wright was to have a major creative role in the production. Not only would he write the screenplay, but after Canada Lee, Wright's first choice for the role of Bigger Thomas, was found to be unavailable, Chenal convinced Wright to play the part himself. In retrospect, Chenal and Wright may have had private doubts about the wisdom of Wright, who was forty years old and had no acting experience, playing the part of an eighteen-year-old lead character in what they hoped would become a widely distributed movie. At the time, however, both men were thrilled with the possibilities posed by their collaboration.

Chenal decided that part of the film should be shot on location in Chicago while the bulk of it would be made in Argentina. Chenal had fled to Argentina during the Nazi occupation of France, and he had connections in the government who were eager to sponsor an artistic undertaking of this magnitude that would be created on Argentine soil. Wright agreed to this arrangement, and on August 20, 1949, he set sail for New York to meet with his agent Paul Reynolds; from there he went on to Chicago to begin filming. He made one more trip to the United States after they finished shooting the film in Argentina. These were the only return visits he was ever to make to his native country.

When he left he planned to be away only for about four months, but due to a number of delays and the relentless perfectionism of the director, the trip extended for almost a year. Wright's long absence was to be a source of strain in his relationship with Ellen. In leaving seven-month-old Rachel, he knew that she would likely regard her father as a stranger when he returned. But he made his concern for his family secondary when he decided to go to Argentina. Since arriving in Paris he had grown frustrated over his inability to focus on his writing, and he found it tempting to blame the distraction posed by his wife and his little girls for his writer's block. He looked forward to being free from the commotion of family life and concentrating on this new creative form.

Working with a personal trainer, Wright lost twenty-five pounds in order to play the role of Bigger. His physical presence had grown throughout the years along with his stature as a writer. His friend C. L. R. James had teasingly told his wife, Constance Webb, that at 170 pounds, his mature weight, Wright looked "bureaucratic," which she claimed was "his new epithet to replace petty-bourgeois." Even after shedding this excess weight, Wright hardly looked the part of an urban teenager. Although Chenal took his job as a director seriously, trying to extract the best possible performance from him, there was little he could do to elevate Wright's amateurish acting ability. Nor could he extract the power of the original *Native Son* from Wright's new script.

Although in some ways Wright remained scrupulously faithful to the novel, he also made changes that altered the dramatic power of his original creation. He toned down the on-screen violence of the book in deference to the sensibilities of the viewing public. He also stripped the film of the strong left-wing political message of the original. During these early years of the cold war, a film glorifying Communist characters could hardly expect to be successful at the box office. Wright's own disillusionment with communism also convinced him to strike many of the polemical passages from the courtroom scene and to portray the character of Jan as merely a "labor organizer" and not a Communist.

Thus, early on, the seeds were planted for an artistic disaster. Still, for the most part Wright enjoyed the process of creating the film. He had a few squabbles with the producers over the terms of his contract and had to hire two different lawyers to represent him. In the end, the film, over budget and destined to perform poorly at the box office, was such a financial failure that there was ultimately little money to fight over. Wright in fact lost money in the project. He did, however, enjoy a rich social life during his months in Argentina. Although he never wrote about his time there, it appears that he enjoyed this reprieve from family life. He did not visit Paris during the duration of the filming, and he would not allow Ellen, who missed her husband desperately, to visit him either. While he was away, his letters home became more infrequent and less loving in tone.

No doubt the primary reason he did not wish to see Ellen was because he developed two romantic attachments while he was away. First, he had a brief affair with Jean Wallace, the twenty-six-year-old blonde actress who played the part of Mary Dalton. After that fling he began seeing Madelyn Jackson, a light-skinned Haitian woman who was an extra in the film. His relationship with Jackson was no fleeting attachment. He even took her to New York with him on the last trip he made to the United States. While there he introduced her to C. L. R. James and Constance Webb in their

Brooklyn apartment. Webb was unimpressed by the scantily clad Jackson, "a woman so desperate for attention that she needed to exhibit her thighs." After leaving New York, the couple went to Haiti together, and Wright began to toy with the idea of living there with Jackson and making a film about Toussaint Louverture, the famed leader of the Haitian Revolution.

He could not, however, delay his return to France indefinitely. At the very least he wanted to be back in Europe to help promote the film there. Upon his arrival he greeted Ellen and the girls coolly, and he admitted to his relationship with Jackson. He told Ellen that if he did not move to Haiti, Jackson would come to Paris. Devastated, Ellen accused Wright of ruining her life, so much of which had been dedicated to supporting his career. Wright was apparently unmoved by his once-beloved wife's emotion as he calmly informed her, "It's your life against mine. I choose mine."

Despite the strength of his passion, Wright's affair with Jackson ended after she became involved with another man. But the damage to Wright's once-loving marriage was irreparable. Eventually Ellen tired of watching with heartbroken bewilderment as her husband consorted with other women, and her attitude toward him changed. Simone de Beauvoir was her chief confidant during this dark period. In her letters to Algren, de Beauvoir reported both on Ellen's initial desolation but also on her eventual ability to reclaim her own life. "She sees Dick with new eyes, discovering he is too selfish. . . . She doesn't love him very much." The couple decided not to divorce and managed to put on a good face in public, but their happiness together was shattered. When Chester Himes arrived in Paris in 1953 after not having seen Ellen for several years, he was shocked by her changed appearance. He had always been attracted to her and was startled to find her "thin and blond, with lots of make-up and a harried, dissatisfied look." Her devotion to Wright had taken an enormous toll on her.

If Wright's marriage was in shambles, the film version of *Native Son* turned out to be a disaster too. Although it had been well received in Argentina, audiences in the United States and Europe were far less favorably impressed. The version that played in the United States was shortened considerably from the original to suit the sensibilities of American censors. Both Wright and Chenal maintained that the editing had ruined their original masterpiece, a claim that likely overstated the quality of the original cut. For both men, the project they had labored on for more than a year was now a colossal embarrassment. Wright put his distress about having created a flop mildly when he said, "My reputation is not being done any good by the film being shown." The combination of events left Wright feeling more miserable and alone than ever. His move to Paris had not soothed his lifelong discontent. Instead it had demonstrated that American racism was no longer the biggest impediment to his happiness. He was, and perhaps always had been, his own greatest enemy. Nonetheless he continued his sojourner's quest for freedom, looking until the end of his life for a place where he could live freely.

CHAPTER SEVEN

Sojourner

ᔧ   During his years in Paris, Wright had become more
aware of the interlocking histories of the people of the African Diaspora. His connection to the Négritude movement
had allowed him to meet many French speakers of African
descent from the Caribbean as well as from the African continent. He had visited Haiti while shooting the film *Native
Son*, gaining some insights into life in the Caribbean. He
began to think more and more about traveling to Africa. His
curiosity was further piqued during the long conversations
with his friend George Padmore, who was deeply involved
in the independence movement in the Gold Coast. When
Wright seriously began considering visiting the continent
in the early 1950s, the Gold Coast was well on its way to
achieving independence from Britain and reincarnating itself as the independent nation of Ghana.

Dorothy Padmore in particular encouraged Wright to
travel to Africa, to the Gold Coast specifically, and to write
about what he observed. Wright later recalled Dorothy's
blunt suggestion, "Now that your desk is clear, why don't
you go to Africa?" Her friendly prodding was all the encouragement he needed. Harpers paid him an advance for a
planned book based on his experiences, which would cover
most of his travel expenses. Padmore then asked Kwame

Nkrumah, prime minister of the emerging nation, to issue
Wright an official invitation to visit the country. After sorting out these logistics, Wright began reading about African
history and culture, and he booked passage on the *Accra*,
which was to leave Liverpool on June 4, 1953.

For Wright, travel was always significant. Because of
his intense nature, he experienced every new place with a
heightened sense of awareness. He was incapable of simply
relaxing and taking in beautiful scenery. Almost maniacally
he endeavored to understand his surroundings and to develop an appreciation for the lives of the people he met. On
every journey he was accompanied by the vague hope that
he would at long last find a sense of belonging, a place where
he could feel at home. Given his predisposition, Wright understandably greeted the idea of visiting the continent of
his ancestors with a complicated array of expectations and
emotions. He wondered, "would I be able to feel and know
something about Africa on the basis of a common 'racial'
heritage?" Furthermore, "Would the Africans regard me as a
long lost brother who had returned?"

Wright's wistful hopefulness that he might find a mys-
tical connection to the people of the Gold Coast vanished
shortly after his arrival. He was fascinated by the mysterious
beauty of the beaches and the inland jungles, and chilled at
the sight of remains of the physical structures that had once
housed slaves bound for North America. He had never been
to a place as densely populated with black people as Accra.
Everyone he saw upon disembarking—from stevedores to
police officers to the engineer of a nearby train—was dark-
skinned. The sight moved him, and he could not help but
be intrigued by the possibilities of being part of a black majority. But he was also alienated by many aspects of life in
West Africa. Although he enjoyed the region's spicy food, it
disagreed with his stomach. He abhorred the tropical heat
and his dingy hotel room. He was appalled by local customs.

A rare photo of Wright with an African family during his trip to the Gold Coast in 1953. He took dozens of photographs during his travels, but he rarely placed himself on the other end of the camera. *(Yale Collection of American Literature, Beinecke Rare Book and Manuscript Library)*

A misplaced homophobia gripped him when he saw African men holding hands. He was horrified by indigenous tribal and religious customs. To his mind, the practice of ancestor worship and the widespread belief in juju that he discovered were ridiculously backward. He was shocked by the different cultural attitude toward public nudity and offended by the sight of the bare breasts of African women. Nearly every aspect of the culture bewildered or offended him.

The Africans that he met more or less reciprocated his ambivalence. They certainly did not regard him as a long lost brother. Kwame Nkrumah was polite but distant, leaving Wright to fend for himself throughout most of the visit.

Many of the Africans he met found Wright's behavior as baffling as he found theirs. Local women laughed at him as he shopped for a cooking pot at the market, performing what they regarded as women's work. Many of the people he met seemed surprised by his frank and forthright manner of interrogation, which must have seemed crass in comparison to the Ghanian preference for indirection and storytelling as a way of conveying information. As Wright wandered around the country wearing his sun helmet and carrying a large camera, his difference was actually inscribed on his person.

Although he had planned to stay in Africa for up to six months, after ten weeks in the country he decided to return to Paris and try to make sense of his experience from there. His account of the trip appeared as *Black Power: A Record of Reactions in a Land of Pathos* in 1954, a perplexing and unstintingly honest book. Traveling to the Gold Coast made Wright realize how deeply Western his own sensibilities were. Although he could find commonality with Africans who had studied or traveled abroad in the United States or in Europe, he felt almost totally alienated from those who clung to their traditional belief system. He was unafraid to say so despite the fact that many black intellectuals, including some of his acquaintances in the Négritude movement, were inclined to romanticize the culture of the continent. Intriguingly, even as he critiqued indigenous African customs he also scrutinized his own reactions with a critical eye. In *Black Power* he decried his own ethnocentrism. He acknowledged "an element of sheer pride in my wanting them to be different. With what god-likeness we all thought of the lives of others!"

Almost paradoxically, in spite of his harsh critique, he felt a deep affection for the people of the Gold Coast and was a strong champion of their right to independence. In

Black Power he urged European powers to allow their colonies to liberate themselves. Because of what he regarded as the primitiveness of the population, however, Wright was unconvinced that the people he met were ready for self-government. Since he did not believe that European powers had a right to govern in Africa, he struggled to find another solution. In a bold letter addressed to Nkrumah himself, he startlingly argued, "AFRICAN LIFE MUST BE MILITARIZED." He believed that Africans like Nkrumah, who had been educated in the West, should temporarily seize control of Africa and operate a heavy-handed civilizing operation from the top down. Later, after being given "organization, direction, meaning, and a sense of justification" by their leaders, the ordinary people would be capable of ruling themselves. Given the history of the postcolonial era, when some African liberation struggles in fact devolved into military dictatorships, Wright's prescription now sounds chilling.

The critical response to this, Wright's first experiment with travel writing, was generally good. He was praised for refusing to romanticize Africa and for his fervent championship of black liberation. George Padmore enjoyed the book as did Walter White, executive secretary of the NAACP. On the other hand, W. E. B. Du Bois resented Wright's scathing analysis of the region's indigenous culture, and most residents of the Gold Coast—including Nkrumah himself—found Wright's portrait extremely unflattering. Of course Wright was no stranger to controversy, but he was not accustomed to writing books, like *Black Power*, that did not sell well. In turning to nonfiction he lost some of his former readers and failed to attract many new ones. The freedom struggles in Africa were simply not a subject that most Americans were concerned about in the mid-1950s.

Despite the mixed results of his trip to Africa and the book he produced, Wright was eager to take on another similar project shortly after his return to Paris. This time, at the suggestion of his friends, the renowned Swedish social scientists and politicians Gunnar and Alva Myrdal, he turned his writerly gaze on Europe. Feeling rootless, Wright saw himself more and more as a citizen of the world, and as such felt a freedom to go where he wished and write about the subjects that interested him. He would not limit his creative efforts to purely racial themes or to peculiarly American ones. Spain intrigued him because it was in many ways set apart from the rest of Europe, ruled by the iron grip of the dictator Francisco Franco. The Spanish Civil War of the 1930s had been a popular cause among American leftists, and Wright knew people who had perished while fighting against Spanish authoritarianism. Traveling to Spain would give him the chance to witness the aftermath of the conflict firsthand.

Wright's response to Spain was nearly as ambivalent as his reaction to Africa. Over the course of three trips in 1954 and 1955 he drove four thousand miles around the country. He felt a greater cultural affinity for the individual Spaniards he met than he had for most of his African acquaintances. He speculated that "Spain had just enough Western aspects of life to make me feel at home." Yet, as in Africa, he was troubled by local religious beliefs. He found the conservative Catholicism practiced in the country to be stultifying and hypocritical. During his travels he was particularly troubled by the poor status of women in Spain. Despite pretensions to religious piety, prostitution flourished throughout the country. Wright was appalled to see women selling their bodies out of economic desperation. He empathized with respectable women too, who were largely confined to their homes. A Spanish acquaintance, André, proudly introduced Wright to his fiancé by proclaiming, "She is a virgin." Wright naively asked, "What does your financée do?" He soon came to understand that, "Being a virgin . . . was a kind of profession in itself."

In *Pagan Spain* (1957), the book that grew out of his travels, Wright compared the plight of women in Spain to the treatment of African Americans in the United States. An American acquaintance of Wright's complained about the discriminatory treatment she had received while traveling in Spain. Her fury prompted him to bluntly tell her, "You are acting like a Negro. Raging and wailing and crying won't help you." This moment of recognition of the commonality between racial discrimination and gender discrimination was a profound moment for him. Newly sensitized to this issue, he later chastised his fellow delegates to the First International Congress of Negro Writers and Artists Conference in 1956 for the underrepresentation of women at the meeting, chiding, "Black men will not be free until their women were free."

Wright was apparently untroubled by a seeming contradiction between his growing consciousness of feminist issues and his own history of stormy relationships with women. Throughout his life he had given himself permission to walk in and out of relationships with women, to enjoy companionship and intimacy when it suited him, and to shun those things when he felt like being alone. His increasingly brazen extramarital affairs also showed a lack of empathy for Ellen, who was hurt and humiliated by her husband's actions. Similarly, Wright's anger about racism and sympathy with its victims did not translate into warm interpersonal relationships with everyone of African descent. Indeed, from his childhood on, Wright had felt peripheral to and critical of many aspects of life in the black community. His love for humanity and outrage against injustice manifested themselves primarily on a broad scale. An advocate for human rights writ large, Wright did not feel compelled to bandage the wounds of each victim of oppression he met. Because he was accustomed to seeing himself as an injured party in the cosmic game of life, he sometimes failed to realize that he too could mete out injustice to others, that he was capable of injuring as well as being hurt.

Nonetheless he had traveled a long way since his days as a "black boy" in Mississippi, and his expanded consciousness allowed him to place his own personal experiences of racial oppression in an ever enlarging frame. When he learned about the 1955 Afro-Asian Conference to be held in Bandung, Indonesia, he was determined to attend. The meeting of African and Asian nations was being called to discuss the international problems of racism and colonialism. Wright was drawn to the event not only because of his identification with oppressed peoples around the globe but because he longed to be part of an international political conversation taking place in an idiom other than that of Marxism. In *The Color Curtain* (1955), his account of the conference, Wright effused that Bandung represented "Something beyond Left and Right."

Wright easily received the funding necessary for this trip from the Congress for Cultural Freedom, an international organization that provided financial support to artists and intellectuals who valued creative as well as political freedom. What Wright did not know at the time was that the organization was bankrolled by the Central Intelligence Agency and was part of an ongoing cultural cold war waged by the American government in an attempt to convince European intellectuals to embrace Americanism rather than communism. Later, when he discovered that the CIA not only funded his trip but also a number of magazines that published his work, Wright was enraged. But in 1955 he was thrilled to have secured the funding to travel to Bandung and to witness what he was certain was the beginning of a new historical era. To Wright, the event "smacked of tidal waves, of natural forces."

Wright's extensive travels during the mid-1950s reflected not only his curiosity about the rest of the world but his growing restlessness in Paris. Ever since he had returned from the shooting of *Native Son* in Argentina, the city had failed to hold the same kind of allure for him. No doubt some of his malaise can be attributed to his degenerating marriage, but it also stemmed from his melancholy nature and from real changes in Parisian social and political life. The Marshall Plan, the U.S.-government-sponsored program to help rebuild war-torn Europe, brought not only American dollars but also many American tourists to the city. With the program came a tremendous American influence, which translated into a diminished racial tolerance. Wright mourned the ill effects of the influx of white Americans in Paris in the pages of *The Crisis* in 1951. The preceding year he had founded an organization called the Franco-American Fellowship, designed to discourage Americans doing business in Paris from bringing attitudes of racial intolerance with them. His efforts met with negligible success. While traveling outside of Paris with Gunnar Myrdal in 1954, the pair were denied admittance to two different hotels. Myrdal interpreted the slights as racism, accusing one hotel clerk of having become "goddamned sophisticated" in an attempt not to offend his American customers.

Living in Paris became even more challenging for Wright and for other African-American expatriates when the Algerian War began in 1954. Most black Americans living in France empathized with the Algerian desire for independence. As guests in the mother country, though, Wright and others knew they dare not speak out publicly against French policies for fear of being expelled. For Wright, who cherished his ability to speak his mind freely, this informal gag order felt oppressive. This was not the kind of freedom he had come to Paris seeking. Still, the fear of being forced to return to the United States to raise his daughters in what he viewed as the hysterical political climate of McCarthyism was enough to effectively silence him, at least on that subject.

The battle against colonialism took place in the already tense cold war atmosphere of the 1950s. Wright had been under the surveillance of the FBI since his first involvement with the Communist party in the 1930s. His activities were scrutinized by the CIA and the State Department as well. As the cold war intensified, he became more aware that he was being spied on. He and other members of the black expatriate community began to worry about who could be trusted. Many of them spotted CIA informers—real or imagined— inside every Paris café. No one seemed more fretful than Wright.

Throughout his life Wright had been wracked with tension. He liked to attribute his anxiety and his boiling rage to his specific environment. He once thought he would become more serene if only he could leave Mississippi, then New York, then the Gold Coast. Now he began having doubts about his life in Paris. He was afraid that some of his acquaintances might be spies who could arrange to have him expelled from France because of his political views. As the decade progressed his thoughts grew more ominous, and he began to worry about his physical safety. He was correct, of course, in his suspicion that the tentacles of the CIA were indeed wrapped around the expatriate community. Wright himself had accepted money from the CIA front, the Congress for Cultural Freedom, and had published his work in *Encounter* and other periodicals that received funding from the agency.

Despite his fears, it seems clear that the CIA was actively promoting Wright's work during this era rather than silencing him. By sponsoring the work of a black *former* Communist, the CIA was boosting the idea of American racial tolerance while helping Wright find an audience for his critique of communism. The American government could not, after all, silence all dissidents and still maintain a credible propaganda war comparing U.S. freedom with Soviet totalitarianism. Instead it would support certain kinds of dissent while keeping an eye on the dissenters. In the 1950s Wright's broadening critiques of international colonialism simply did not hit quite as close to home as his earlier indictments of American society as set forth in *Uncle Tom's Children, Native Son,* and *Black Boy.*

Wright had been surveyed by American intelligence agencies for most of his adult life, but there is no direct evidence that this scrutiny intensified near the end of his life. Trying to gauge the factual basis of his obsessive fear is difficult. Of course clandestine activities like spying are designed not to leave traces for the historian to analyze. Near the end of his life Wright certainly believed he was in greater peril than ever before, a suspicion that cannot be confirmed from his FBI file alone. It reveals that the intelligence community vacillated in their assessment of the risk posed by their subject. In 1947 the bureau proposed ending its surveillance of Wright because he was no longer a party member, noting in 1948 that "subject was definitely not of a Marxist frame of mind." But other FBI documents speculated that he might have been more sympathetic to party aims than his public disavowals suggested. In 1951 an informant claimed that Wright "is as much a Communist as he has ever been."

Regardless of his political leanings, during the 1950s it was clear that Wright's influence as a writer had waned. He

still inspired international admiration for his past achievements, and he continued to command great respect in French
literary and intellectual circles. But his latest books did not
sell well, particularly in the United States. Thus it seems
somewhat doubtful that the U.S. government regarded
Wright as a greater threat than ever before. That was, however, Wright's perception. He felt as if he were under siege.
Writing in 1960, shortly before his death, he complained, "I
lift my hand to fight Communism and I find that the hand of
the Western world is sticking knives into my back."

His reaction to the cold war was colored by his personality. His fellow black expatriate writer Chester Himes
claimed that Wright was generally prone to "such self-indulgent exaggeration that the buzzing of a blowfly could
rage like a typhoon in his imagination." In his heightened
state of anxiety, he found reasons for concern everywhere.
A dispute between Wright's closest friend in the black expatriate community, the cartoonist Ollie Harrington, and
the African-American journalist Richard Gibson helped fuel
his suspicions about a widespread conspiracy. The conflict
began when Harrington, who planned to spend some time in
Sweden, sublet his Paris apartment to Gibson. When Harrington returned, Gibson refused to give up the apartment.
Gibson later claimed this was because Harrington was behind on his rent, and his own occupancy was contingent
upon an agreement with the landlord not to relinquish the
apartment to Harrington. Not only did Gibson fail to vacate the apartment, Harrington later claimed that he also
refused to let him remove his furniture and paintings from
the space. Harrington was in a difficult position. Because he
was well known for his left-wing politics, he was reluctant
to complain to the authorities for fear of having his passport
revoked. He abandoned the apartment to Gibson but tried
to settle the score by getting the best of him in a fistfight
outside the Café Tournon.

Not long after the scuffle, on October 21, 1957, Harrington was horrified to read a letter to the editor in *Life*
magazine critical of French policy toward Algeria, which
was signed "Ollie Harrington." Worried about his immigra-
tion status, he went to the authorities to disavow writing
the letter. A police investigation revealed that it had actually been written by Richard Gibson, who later claimed that
he wrote it merely to publicize the Algerian situation. Harrington and Wright regarded Gibson's motives as far more
sinister, believing that he aimed to get Harrington deported.
In Wright's mind this episode was evidence that the black
expatriate community had been infiltrated by a dubious element and that neither he nor Harrington was safe.

His suspicions were further aroused in 1958 when an
article about black expatriates, "Among the Alien Corn,"
appeared in *Time* magazine. Wright was quoted as saying
that the racial situation in America "had not changed in 300
years." Although he probably agreed with that statement, he
angrily claimed that he had not made it and in fact had not
even been interviewed by the magazine. He sent a furious
telegram to the editors at *Time*, accusing them of "character
assassination." He was similarly horrified in 1960 when he
received a postcard sent to him by Gibson from Cuba, inviting him to visit a "land that has dared shake off the shack-
les of American imperialism." Was Gibson trying to damage
Wright's reputation by associating him with postrevolution-
ary Cuba? He felt perpetually under assault.

Ironically, some members of the black community suspected that Wright, in spite of his obvious paranoia about
surveillance, was himself working for the U.S. government.
In 1956 the American writer Kay Boyle wrote to Wright
telling him that a rumor was circulating in left-wing circles
in the United States that he worked for either the FBI or the
State Department, passing on information about other expatriates in exchange for being able to keep his passport. Wright

was no doubt embarrassed to hear these rumors, but his relationship with American officials in Paris was at times cozier than he let on. For example, during the planning stages of the 1956 First International Conference of Negro Writers and Artists, he voluntarily went to the American Embassy to express his concerns about the possibility of Communist influence at the meeting, asking officials there to help him recruit black American delegates who did not hold Communist sympathies. Wright, of course, had to remain mute about his intervention when the conference finally opened and a letter was read from the venerable W. E. B. Du Bois who, though invited, was unable to attend because he had been denied a passport. Wright resented Du Bois's claim that the only Americans who were allowed to travel abroad were those who were willing to censor themselves in accordance with government demands.

Throughout the meeting Wright emphatically denied that anyone was hindering his freedom of speech. Indeed there is no reason to suspect that he felt obliged to censor himself. In his speech at the conference he told a stunned audience that some of the consequences of colonialism had been good. The nations of Africa and Asia should be grateful for their exposure to Western ideas. He acknowledged that many of the fruits of colonialism had been bitter, and he regretted that Europeans could not have gone about their civilizing mission "out of generosity of heart" rather than out of greed. But he thought that developing countries should nonetheless thank the West for helping free them from the "stultifying traditions" of their native cultures. Needless to say, this was not a popular point of view in the assembly.

Wright's moodiness, his paranoia, and his increasingly unorthodox political ideas all conspired to make him feel increasingly alienated in Paris. As he aged he had fewer and fewer friends. In some settings, mostly in French circles, he was feted as a grand American writer, but in other contexts, particularly among the expatriate community, he was often met with hostility. Through the decade he grew apart from Chester Himes, whose literary career had thrived in Paris. He struck Himes as increasingly "spiteful and critical." Wright's friend Ollie Harrington recalled that some regulars at the Café Tournon relished quarreling with Wright, "referring to his books and opinions with contempt." As the years went by, Wright spent more time alone playing the pinball machine at Tournon while many younger African-American writers refused even to acknowledge his presence in the café. This strained dynamic stood in contrast to his early years in Paris when he seemed to be at the center of every conversation.

Strangely, even when Wright was in some ways on the periphery of things, he still inhabited the imaginary center of the black expatriate community in Paris. His success as a writer—though diminishing year by year—remained unrivaled. He had created the role of the world-famous African-American writer. Others who would follow in his footsteps, including Ralph Ellison, Chester Himes, and James Baldwin, owed some of their success to Wright's early encouragement. After Wright's death, Baldwin reflected that Wright "had never really been a human being for me, he had been an idol." Because of his enormous stature in the world of international letters, because of the sheer scale of his success, Baldwin—and by extension others—failed to recognize the extent of Wright's frailty.

Baldwin gained insights into the inner workings of the renowned writer the hard way. He had first met Wright in Brooklyn in 1945 at the age of twenty, at which time he was starstruck to be in the presence of the author of *Uncle Tom's Children* and *Native Son*. Wright, who often served as a generous mentor to less-established writers, immediately recognized the young man's talent and helped him secure a fellowship that enabled him to work on his first novel, which was finally published in 1953 as *Go Tell It on the Mountain*. Baldwin continued to follow in his mentor's footsteps by relocating to Paris in 1948. Their relationship there, however, got off to a rocky start after Baldwin's essay "Everybody's Protest Novel" appeared in *Zero* magazine in 1949. In the piece, Baldwin compares *Native Son* to the classic melodramatic abolitionist novel *Uncle Tom's Children* by Harriet Beecher Stowe. Both books, he argued, were polemics that denied their black characters a humanity that transcended stereotypes.

Not understanding Wright's psyche, Baldwin had expected his mentor to be proud of him for his original ideas and to accept the ascendancy of a new generation of black writers who would see the world differently from their literary forefather. Had not Wright himself been critical of many of the writers of the Harlem Renaissance? Wright, however, was stunned and felt betrayed by Baldwin's public critique of his work. Sometime in May 1953 the pair had a famous falling-out in a Paris café, observed by a very uncomfortable Chester Himes. Wright accused Baldwin of ingratitude, and Baldwin passionately defended his right to have his own literary viewpoint, declaring "The sons must slay their fathers." From that point on, Wright deliberately saw very little of this man who had so aggressively claimed him as a father.

Wright felt increasingly beleaguered during the 1950s. He had weathered a severe dry spell in his creative output during his first years in exile, and his new work, his experimental nonfiction, had not been commercially successful. Meanwhile his literary protégés seemed poised to pass him by. Ralph Ellison won the National Book Award for his 1953 novel *Invisible Man*, a virtuoso performance that many hailed as the best novel ever written by an African-American writer. Closer to home in Paris, Himes was producing well-received novels at a breakneck pace. Taking account, Wright decided it was time for him to return to his roots, to the formula that had made him so successful. He would write another novel about racism in the United States.

The Long Dream (1958) was set in a small town in Mississippi. The protagonist, Fishbelly Tucker, is the son of Tyree, a corrupt black undertaker who can afford a comfortable lifestyle from his involvement in prostitution and gambling. Tyree stays in business by bribing the local police chief, who later has him killed to silence him about the white establishment's involvement in these criminal activities. In the aftermath of his father's murder, Fishbelly flees Mississippi for Paris. Once again Wright grapples with the recurrent theme from his earlier fiction of the struggle to develop a masculine identity in a world where black men are infantilized. The specter of the white woman that haunted many of Wright's earlier protagonists also reappears in this novel. Fishbelly is tormented by both the allure and the consequences of interracial sex. For a time he carries around a picture of a white woman torn from a newspaper, and he dates Gladys, a prostitute who could pass for white.

Ed Aswell, Wright's favorite editor who was now working at Doubleday, offered him a contract for the new book. He was thrilled that Wright had returned to the material that had first made him so successful. For years he had worried that Wright, by leaving the country, had lost the chief source of his literary power, the strain he felt living as a black man in the United States. Paul Reynolds too had worried about the impact that expatriation had had on his client's work, but he thought the new novel was Wright's best piece of writing in many years. Both men thought Wright's unwieldy manuscript needed work. It had to be shortened considerably, and much of the vulgar language needed to be cleaned up, but they were optimistic and encouraging. When the novel was published, the critics were less than enthusiastic about the results of Wright's labor.

One of the most often repeated refrains in the reviews was that Wright had indeed lost touch with life in the United States. He had been away too long, and he did not recognize the changes being wrought by the civil rights movement. Wright, however, was not prepared to agree with white liberal critics who thought the South had changed drastically since the days of his own childhood in Mississippi. News reports of violent white resistance to school desegregation in places like Little Rock certainly seemed to confirm Wright's skepticism. He was continually bewildered by the criticism he received for leaving the country, both from those who thought he had now forfeited his right to comment on the American scene and from those who thought he had betrayed his people by fleeing the United States instead of staying and fighting. White expatriates, he believed, were not exposed to the same level of scrutiny.

Concerns for the reception of his writing were now compounded by new anxieties about his health. In August 1956 he had become seriously ill and was admitted to the hospital for amoebic dysentery, a condition he probably picked up from tainted food or water during the course of his travels. From this point on, he would never fully regain his health. Throughout his life Wright had suffered on and off from stomach ailments and with bouts of what he called grippe. His complaints about one malady or another were frequent enough that many of his closest friends accused him of hypochondria. Because of his history of minor health problems, few in his circle appreciated the gravity of his condition or dreamed that he would die four short years after this latest diagnosis.

In the midst of his malaise, and in spite of his physical weakness, Wright began to contemplate leaving Paris, continuing his lifelong pattern of seeking to fill his internal void with an external change of scenery. The political situation in Paris was tense, and he had grown weary of the intrigue in the black expatriate circle. He was not willing to return to the United States, but in 1957, as he was finishing work on *The Long Dream*, he began to think about moving to London and starting a new life there. In addition to his restlessness, family considerations also prompted the idea of relocation. Ellen had begun working as a literary agent and counted Simone de Beauvoir and Chester Himes among her clients. She enjoyed her work and thought she might be able to attract more clients in England. Julia had decided to attend university at Cambridge, where she could study in her native tongue.

In 1959, Ellen and the girls went to London to look for a place to live. Wright planned to follow, but British officials refused him permission to reside there permanently, offering him only a visitor's visa, which would allow him to stay in the country for a one-year trial period. Feeling persecuted, Wright was unwilling to relocate under those terms. He would stay in France while Ellen and the girls lived in London. Living in separate countries made the troubles in the Wright marriage much more visible, but the pair agreed not to divorce for the sake of appearances and out of love for their children.

Maintaining two separate households further strained Wright's steadily diminishing financial resources. The large bank account he had amassed when *Black Boy* was a best-seller had provided most of the money he had used to support his family for the past decade, and now these funds were nearly depleted. Because his more recent books had sold poorly, the Wright family could no longer live in the style they were accustomed to. Reluctantly, Wright decided to sell his writer's retreat, a farmhouse he and Ellen had purchased in Normandy in 1955. He also sold the family residence on rue Monsieur le Prince, replacing it with a one-bedroom apartment on the nearby rue Régis, where he would live alone for the rest of his life. Despite these attempts at economy, in September 1960 the once-prosperous writer had less than a thousand dollars in his bank account.

Wright's new apartment was small but comfortable. The focal point of the sitting area was a large divan covered in emerald green velour. The walls of the apartment seemed to be covered entirely with books. Wright appreciated his solitude, and in spite of his frail health he wrote prolifically. By 1959 he had completed a four-hundred-page sequel to *The Long Dream*, which he was calling "Island of Hallucinations." The novel follows the character Fishbelly to Paris, where he meets a cast of characters that bear striking resemblances to many members of the black expatriate community that Wright knew. Using the guise of fiction, Wright creates unflattering portraits of James Baldwin, Richard Gibson, Chester Himes, and William Gardner Smith, among others. The only character who fares well in the novel, Ned Harrison, seems to be based on Ollie Harrington.

Although writing the book may have been therapeutic for Wright, his editor on the project, Tim Seldes of Doubleday, was unsure of its literary merits. He asked Wright for substantial revisions that were never made. Instead Wright began to work on another novel, published posthumously in 2008 as *A Father's Law*. One of its main characters abandons his fiancée when he learns that she has congenital syphilis, much as Wright himself had done decades earlier. Clearly Wright spent much of the last months of his life in deep reflection about his past experiences and the choices he had made.

He now wrote almost every morning in spite of his illness. He went out less frequently, often eating at home where he continued to enjoy cooking his own food. His last romantic relationship was with Celia Hornung, a German-Jewish woman who had managed to escape from the Nazis in the 1940s and was now living in Paris. Although she found Wright intriguing, she never fell in love with him. Their affair was quiet and lacking in passion. Hornung was not interested in nursing Wright through his illness or in boosting his spirits as his struggle with depression deepened. She found his manners crude, and she was not particularly impressed with his writing. The affair ended when Hornung left Paris to visit another lover in Australia. Upon her departure, Wright's solitude deepened.

His closest confidant during the last months of his life was Margrit de Sablonière, who lived in Holland and who had translated several of Wright's books into Dutch. Most of their friendship took place by correspondence. Their early letters are formal but friendly and concerned primarily with the nuances involved in translating literary work. Slowly, however, they dropped the pretense of business and began addressing each other by first names and discussing personal issues, particularly Wright's health. More than anyone else, de Sablonière knew the details of Wright's mental state and of his illness. She fretted about him, sent him care packages, and took his anxiety seriously. It was to her that he sent the ominous letter that has since become part of the lore surrounding his death. He told her, "I don't want anything to happen to me, but if it does, my friends will know exactly where it comes from." In his last months of life, Wright felt that his life was in danger and that he might be killed by an American government belatedly angry over his publications about Africa and Bandung.

Another omnipresent fixture in his life during this period was his doctor, Vladimir Schwarzmann, a Russian gastroenterologist who began treating him in February 1960. The doctor was a fan of Wright's work and agreed not to charge him for his services, an arrangement that struck some of Wright's friends as peculiar. He put Wright on a bland diet and ordered him to abstain from alcohol. He also prescribed various medications and vitamin shots and had Wright take daily doses of bismuth salts, which were to serve as an antacid. Under his care, Wright conquered the amoebas, but he never regained his strength and continued to suffer from a variety of symptoms. He grew increasingly feeble and was prone to exhaustion. He had frequent nausea and diarrhea, causing him to lose weight.

As he struggled to recover, Wright developed an intense friendship with Schwarzmann. They even traveled to Holland together, where they spent time with de Sablonière, who disliked the doctor immediately. Schwarzmann was cool to her, and she thought that Wright behaved uneasily in his presence. Wright admitted to her later that something about the doctor did make him feel tense and uneasy, but he chided himself for his suspicions. Dorothy Padmore met Schwarzmann during a brief trip to Paris, and she too found something curious about him. She wondered how the doctor could afford his opulent apartment when he seemed to have very few patients. Both de Sablonière and Padmore feared that Wright was taking too many drugs, and that his treatments were doing more harm than good. Julia, who had decided to return to Paris to be near her sick father while studying at the Sorbonne, had similar concerns. Near the end of Wright's life, when she went to the pharmacy to pick up a prescription for him, the pharmacist warned her that he was taking far too much medication.

The collective suspicions of these three people who cared for Wright may have indeed been correct. Wright's biographer Hazel Rowley has suggested that he may have been suffering from bismuth poisoning. Although little was known about the side effects of oral bismuth during Wright's life, it is now recognized that high doses of the drug can lead to a variety of complications and even to death through kidney or liver failure. All of Wright's physical symptoms during the last months of his life are consistent with bismuth poisoning, and his emotional state too may have been affected by the drug. Both depression and paranoia have been linked to overdoses of bismuth.

As Wright's health failed and he struggled to keep his spirits up, he was distraught to learn of the deaths of many of the people he most loved and admired. His Aunt Maggie, the only member of his extended family whom he had kept in touch with throughout the years, died in 1957. His favorite editor and close friend Ed Aswell passed away suddenly in 1958. Both his friend George Padmore and his mother died in 1959. Padmore had been a staunch supporter of Wright's work and his major link to the struggle against colonialism in Africa, a cause that Wright cared deeply about. Even in the midst of his illness he had begun planning a trip to French-speaking Africa that was to take place when he was strong enough to travel. The death of his mother also came as a blow. Although it had been years since Wright had seen her, he faithfully sent her money every month and thought about her tenderly.

Wright consoled himself in the face of his declining health and this steady stream of bad news in an unexpected way. He began writing haiku. He was introduced to the form by an acquaintance, the South African poet Sinclair Beiles, in 1959. Wright met Beiles and several other writers associated with the Beat Generation at a hotel bar near his rue Régis apartment. This fortuitous encounter exposed Wright to a poetic language that proved to be good therapy for him. In the eighteen months before his death, he composed more than four thousand of these tiny poems, which contained only seventeen syllables each. As in classical haiku, many of Wright's poems strive to capture an image from the natural world. Most were inspired by the French countryside; others seem to invoke memories from his world travels or the landscape of his Mississippi childhood. With their spare use of words and their rigid format, these meditative poems allowed Wright to impose structure on a universe that had spiraled out of control. They reflect both his continual wonder at the beauty of the world and his precarious physical and emotional state. As if anticipating his death while commenting on his mental state, he wrote:

> I am nobody:
> A red sinking autumn sun
> Took my name away.

When death finally came to Wright, he was not expecting it. On November 26, 1960, at Schwarzmann's urging, he checked into the nearby Eugene Gibez Clinic for a checkup and rest following a series of dizzy spells. This was his first experience at the clinic. In the past he had always been treated at the American Hospital. As he prepared to make his way to the clinic, his daughter Julia was with him. They were surprised when the doorbell rang and their unexpected visitor turned out to be Langston Hughes. Ushered into the tiny apartment, Hughes was surprised to see how ill Wright appeared. He was consoled, though, when Wright began talking animatedly, charming Hughes with his familiar smile. Throughout his life he retained the ability to temporarily conceal his anxieties and his illnesses, suddenly breaking into the uproarious laugh that his friends knew so well. On his way out the door, Wright gave Hughes a copy of a manuscript he had been working on, promising to write soon.

He appeared to be in good spirits after arriving at the clinic. The nurse recalled that shortly after his arrival he had a female visitor, whose identity remains uncertain. He spoke to Ellen on the telephone and gave her no reason for special concern. On the evening of November 28 he rang the bell by his bed for assistance. By the time the nurse reached him, he was dead. Official records indicate that he died of a heart attack at 11 PM, fewer than two months after his fifty-second birthday. In spite of his poor health, no one had seen this coming. Ollie Harrington was among the first to get the news. He had telephoned the clinic after receiving a mysterious telegram from Wright asking him to come see him immediately. Harrington was stunned to discover that he had answered his friend's urgent message too late.

Wright's funeral on December 3 was a small, hastily arranged affair. Ellen and Julia attended while Rachel, who had always had a strained and distant relationship with her father, waited in the car. News of his death did not reach Wright's seemingly infinite list of acquaintances in time for most to attend the funeral. Harrington and Chester Himes were there along with a handful of others. Thomas Diop, one of Wright's friends from the Présence Africaine group, spoke briefly. It was a surprisingly small and quiet commemoration of such a large personality. But news of Wright's death soon elicited waves of regret and nostalgia among a lifetime of friends and admirers.

Even though her friendship with Wright had ended decades earlier, when Margaret Walker heard the news she "felt as if a relative had passed away." James Baldwin's ambivalent fascination with Wright only intensified after his death, and he came to consider Wright's work, which he had once criticized, to be "an irreducible part of the history of our swift and terrible time." For Ralph Ellison, Wright's passing marked a milestone in his own existence. He realized that "a period of my own life has come to a definite end." Horace Cayton, once one of Wright's dearest friends, channeled his grief over losing Wright into the project of writing a biography of his friend. Cayton met his own death in 1970 while conducting research on Wright's life in Paris. John A. Williams very publicly reflected on the meaning of Wright's life and death in his 1967 roman à clef, *The Man Who Cried I Am*. The plot of the novel centers on the mysterious death of Harry Ames, an internationally famous and deeply flawed black writer who lives in Paris and is married to a white woman. His resemblance to Wright is unmistakable.

Given the suddenness of his death and Wright's certainty near the end of his life that he had enemies who wished to harm him, rumors have persisted that Wright did not die of natural causes. Who was the mysterious woman who visited him shortly before his died? Why did he send an urgent telegram to Ollie Harrington asking him to visit? What precisely was the nature of his relationship to Schwarzmann? Why did he go to the small Eugene Gibez Clinic and not to the American Hospital where he usually received his care? Why was he so certain that he was in danger? Ollie Harrington and Julia Wright both suspected foul play and the involvement of an organization such as the CIA or the FBI in Wright's sudden death. Others speculated that the intelligence agencies were at best only partially responsible. Knowing that he was being watched certainly added to Wright's anxiety during the last months of his life, and one would be hard pressed to argue that his tense mental state did not contribute to his ongoing health problems. Still, he had always suffered anxiety throughout his life. Bismuth poisoning presents yet another possibility. Because Ellen did not order an autopsy, a definitive answer to the precise cause of death will never be known.

Wright could scarcely have written a more dramatic ending for his own life if he had tried. His last book project, *A Father's Law*, left unfinished at the time of his death, was a thriller. The plot of the novel concerns a series of unexplained murders—left eternally unresolved with Wright's passing. It may have given him some pleasure had he known that his own ending would be equally mysterious, that his death as well as his life would be a source of consternation for his devoted fans as well as his critics. In the end it is somehow fitting that an eternal mystery lingers over a man whose literary crusade for social justice often came wrapped inside the guise of the dark and sinister plots that haunted his ever-active imagination.

The sad occasion of Wright's death was not the only time when the plots of his fiction and his life collided. Anyone familiar with Wright's life and his work will recognize glimpses of the man in his fictional creations. The Southern black characters in *Uncle Tom's Children* offer insights into the author's sincere hope that collective, biracial activism might actually help create a better world. In Bigger Thomas we gain a deeper sense of the depth of Wright's own insecurities and fears. In the form of Cross Damon we see an incarnation of Wright's introspective nature and catch frightening glimpses of his dark, selfish side. Through Fishbelly's fictional life we see Wright's belief that travel furthers intellectual and emotional freedom. Collectively these characters have earned their creator immortality.

Wright never solved the nagging question of his life: how best to live freely. He never found the peace and contentment he sought. He did, however, overcome the obscure origins he derided so convincingly in *Black Boy*. Following the example of H. L. Mencken, who taught him to use words as weapons, he repeatedly met his objective of shocking his readers into thinking about global issues of social justice in different and unconventional ways, in the process altering the history of American letters.

Acknowledgments

THIS BOOK bears the imprint of two outstanding editors. I could not ask for a better editor, mentor, or friend than John David Smith. It was an enormous privilege to work with him on this project. I am also grateful to Ivan Dee for his frank and careful editing. He taught me a great deal about the craft of writing. The Georgia College & State University Foundation provided the funding necessary to travel to the Beinecke Library to examine Wright's papers; I am thankful for its support. Michelle Flirt, a graduate student at GCSU, compiled a useful bibliography of criticism of Wright's later works. Through the years John Ferling has offered me sound advice on the technique of writing history for a general audience rather than for a mere handful of specialists. After he reads this book, I hope he will find his efforts rewarded. Lindsey Swindall has been a valuable confidant and sounding board at every stage of this project. I am grateful to my new colleagues at the University of North Texas for welcoming me with open arms and for offering so much collective wisdom on the art of doing history. My first and most important reader remains my mother, Carolyn S. Briggs. Finally, thank you to Charles Bittner, who lived with this

project every day and who also took the plunge of following
my career to Texas.

                                              J. J. W.

Denton, Texas
January 2010

A Note on Sources

RICHARD WRIGHT has been the subject of several book-length biographies. Michel Fabre's *The Unfinished Quest of Richard Wright* (New York, 1973) combines extensive biographical information with sensitive readings of Wright's major works. To date the most definitive biography is Hazel Rowley's *Richard Wright: The Life and Times* (New York, 2001). In this meticulously researched book, Rowley unearths much previously unknown information. She is particularly skilled at describing Wright's romantic life. Much of my understanding of Wright's character is derived from Rowley's interpretation. I owe a great debt to both Rowley and Fabre; each chapter of this short biography bears the imprint of their pioneering efforts. Addison Gayle's Richard *Wright: Ordeal of a Native Son* (New York, 1980) offers a particularly careful reading of Wright's FBI file. His former friend Margaret Walker's *Richard Wright: Daemonic Genius* (New York, 1988) inspired a lawsuit by the Wright estate, which unsuccessfully sued Walker for quoting liberally from his unpublished works. Walker describes Wright as a tortured genius who grappled with a number of demons including, she intimates, some sexual issues. Her youthful, unrequited romantic attachment to Wright may have colored her interpretation. Another friend, Constance Webb, published *Richard Wright: A Biography* (New York, 1968) a mere eight years after his death. Although the book contains many interesting anecdotes, it is riddled with factual errors that were later corrected by Fabre and Rowley.

While writing this biography of Wright I consulted the vast collection of Richard Wright Papers at Yale University's Beinecke Library. This treasure trove of material includes voluminous correspondence, Wright's journals, and hundreds of pages of both published and unpublished manuscripts. I also examined the Wright materials housed at the Schomburg Center for Research in Black Culture in Harlem.

The Richard Wright Encyclopedia (Westport, Conn., 2008), edited by Jerry W. Ward, Jr., and Robert J. Butler, is the most comprehensive single resource about Wright's life and his literary works. Wright has been the subject of a seemingly endless array of books, dissertations, and articles. It would be impossible to do justice to the field of Wright scholarship here. Readers interested in learning more about Wright's work should consult two important bibliographies, both compiled by the late Keneth Kinnamon. The first volume, *A Richard Wright Bibliography* (Jefferson, N.C., 1988), covers the years 1933 through 1982 and contains 13,117 citations. Volume two, *Richard Wright: An Annotated Bibliography of Criticism and Commentary, 1983–2003*, contains another 8,660 entries.

Among the best sources of information about Wright are his own writings, several of which contain explicitly autobiographical material. Because Wright was so prolific, it is impractical to attempt to document each publication in this short biography. What follows is a list of his major works (several of which were published posthumously) in chronological order:

"Blueprint for Negro Writing," *New Challenge,* Fall 1937, 53–65

Uncle Tom's Children: Four Novellas (New York, 1938)

Uncle Tom's Children: Five Long Stories (New York, 1940)

Native Son (New York, 1940)

Native Son: The Biography of a Young American: A Play in Ten Scenes. With Paul Green. (New York, 1941)

"How Bigger Was Born" (pamphlet) (New York, 1941)

Twelve Million Black Voices (New York, 1941)

"I Tried to Be a Communist," *Atlantic Monthly,* August 1944, 61–70

Black Boy: A Record of Childhood and Youth (New York, 1945)

The Outsider (New York, 1953)

Savage Holiday (New York, 1954)

Black Power: A Record of Reactions in a Land of Pathos (New York, 1954)

The Color Curtain: A Report on the Bandung Conference (Cleveland, Ohio, 1956)

Pagan Spain (New York, 1957)

White Man, Listen! (New York, 1957)

The Long Dream (New York, 1958)

Eight Men (Cleveland, Ohio, 1961)
Lawd Today! (New York, 1963)
American Hunger (New York, 1977)
Rite of Passage (New York, 1994)
Haiku: This Other World (New York, 1988)
A Father's Law (New York: 2008)

Chapter One: Black Boy

Leon Litwack's Pulitzer Prize–winning study, *Been in the Storm So Long: The Aftermath of Slavery* (New York, 1980), brings to life the tumultuous world that Wright's grandparents inhabited after emancipation. James Cobb's *The Most Southern Place on Earth: The Mississippi Delta and the Roots of Regional Identity* (New York, 1994) movingly describes the grim realities of life in the Jim Crow Mississippi of his childhood. Nan Woodruff's *American Congo: The African-American Freedom Struggle in the Delta* (Cambridge, Mass., 2003) crosses the Mississippi River and offers descriptions of life in Arkansas during the same period. *Under Sentence of Death: Lynching in the South* (Chapel Hill, 1997), edited by W. Fitzhugh Brundage, offers insights into the culture of violence during the era of segregation. Jennifer Ritterhouse's innovative study, *Growing Up Jim Crow: The Racial Socialization of Black and White Southern Children, 1890–1940* (Chapel Hill, 2006), is a good source for learning more about how children like Wright learned the intricate rules of Southern racism. Readers interested in finding out more about Wright's Memphis should consult *Memphis in Black and White* (Mount Pleasant, S.C., 2003) by Beverly Bond and Janann Sherman, and *African Americans in Memphis* (Mount Pleasant, S.C., 2009) by Earnestine Lovelle Jenkins. *Goin' Back to Memphis: A Century of Blues, Rock 'n' Roll, and Glorious Soul*, by James Dickerson (New York, 1996) provides information about the blues music scene, which was centered on Beale Street near the Wright family's home.

Chapter Two: Refugee

Land of Hope: Chicago, Black Southerners, and the Great Migration (Chicago, 1991) by James R. Grossman provides the historical

context for the next phase of Wright's journey. For more information about African-American life during the Great Depression,
see *To Ask for an Equal Chance: African Americans in the Great
Depression* (New York, 2009) by Cheryl Greenberg. A number of
books supplied me with important details about the activities of
the Communist party during this period, including *Red Chicago:
American Communism at Its Grassroots, 1928–35* (Champaign,
Ill., 2007) by Randi Storch; *Black Marxism: The Making of the
Black Radical Tradition* (London, 1983) by Cedric J. Robinson; *The
Communist Party in the United States: From the Great Depres-
sion to World War II* (New Brunswick, N.J., 1991) by Fraser M. Ot-
tonelli; and most notably *Exiles from a Future Time: The Forging
of the Mid-Twentieth Century Literary Left* (Chapel Hill, 2001) by
Alan M. Wald.

Chapter Three: Breakthrough

David A. Taylor's *Soul of a People: The WPA Writers' Project Uncovers Depression America* (New York, 2009) and Jerrold Hirsch's
*Portrait of America: A Cultural History of the Federal Writers'
Project* (Chapel Hill, 2006) are good sources for learning more
about the Federal Writers' Project. David Levering Lewis's *When
Harlem Was in Vogue* (New York, 1997) provides useful background reading for understanding the generation of black writers
that proceeded Wright. Gilbert Osofsky's *Harlem: The Making of
a Ghetto* (New York, 1966) and Jervis Anderson's *This Was Harlem: A Cultural Portrait, 1900–1950* (New York, 1982) offer detailed descriptions of the neighborhood that Wright wrote about
for both the *Daily Worker* and the Federal Writers' Project. For
more information about Wright's literary contemporaries, see *The
New Red Negro: The Literary Left and African-American Poetry,
1930–1946* by James E. Smethurst (New York, 1999). When Wright
turned from poetry to prose, his writing was infused with his interest in sociology. For background reading on this subject, see *The
Chicago School of Sociology* by Martin Blumer (Chicago, 1986).
Arnold Rampersand's masterful *Ralph Ellison: A Biography* (New
York, 2008) does an admirable job of documenting Wright's closest
male friendship during this period. I consulted several books to better understand the culture of the Communist party in New York,
including *Communists in Harlem During the Great Depression* by

Mark Naison (Champaign, Ill., 2004); *New Negro, Old Left: African American Writing and Communism Between the Wars* by William J. Maxwell (New York, 1999); and *Black Liberation/Red Scare: Ben Davis and the Communist Party* by Gerald Horne (Newark, Del., 1994). Each contains insights into the interracial marriage and dating that were prevalent in the party.

Chapter Four: Marriage

Insights into Wright's relationship with Margaret Walker may be found not only in her biography of Wright but also in *How I Wrote Jubilee: And Other Essays on Life and Literature* (New York, 1990). *The Diary of Anais Nin, Volume Three, 1939–1944* (San Diego, 1969), edited by Gunther Stuhlman, provides short snapshots of Wright during the early days of his marriage to Ellen. Constance Webb's memoir *Not Without Love* (Danvers, Mass., 2003) contains, among other things, information about Wright's friendship with her husband C. L. R. James.

Chapter Five: Fame

Readers may find more information about the theatrical production of *Native Son* and about Wright's collaborators in the project in *Orson Welles: Volume 1: The Road to Xanadu* by Simon Callow (New York, 1997); *Paul Green: Playwright of the Real South* by John Herbert Roper (Athens, Ga., 2003); and *Unfinished Business: Memoirs, 1902–1988* by John Houseman (London, 1986). *NAACP: A History of the National Association for the Advancement of Colored People* by Charles Kellogg Flint (Baltimore, 1967) offers an overview of the history of the organization that in 1941 awarded Wright its prestigious Spingarn Medal. For more details on why Wright left the Communist party, see his essay in *The God That Failed* (New York, 1949), edited by Richard Crossman. *Double Victory: A Multicultural History of America in World War II* (Boston, 2001) by Ronald Takaki explains the dilemma that African Americans like Wright felt during World War II when they were asked to fight in a segregated army. *Long Old Road: An Autobiography* (Seattle, Wash., 1965) by Horace R. Cayton, Jr., offers some descriptions of Cayton's friendship with Wright. *A History of Fisk University, 1865–1946* (Tuscaloosa, Ala., 2002) by Joe A. Richardson gives a history of the institution where Wright gave the talk that inspired him to write his autobiography *Black Boy*. A series of letters between Wright and a childhood friend, *Letters to Joe C. Brown* (Kent, Ohio, 1968), edited by Thomas Knipp, reveal something about Wright's state of mind after he began to enjoy success as a writer.

Chapter Six: Expatriate

Tyler Stovall's *Paris Noir: African Americans in the City of Light* (New York, 1996) offers an excellent overview of the black expatriate scene in Paris. *Exiled in Paris: Richard Wright, James Baldwin, Samuel Beckett, and Others on the Left Bank* (New York, 1995) by James Campbell provides an illuminating description of Wright's experiences in his adopted city. Readers interested in learning more about Gertrude Stein's famous salon may read *Charmed Circle: Gertrude Stein and Company* by James R. Mellow (New York, 1974). An overview of the thought of Jean-Paul Sartre and his contemporaries, whom Wright found so influential, may be found in *Sartre's French Contemporaries and Enduring Influence* (New York, 1996) by William McBride. *Black Writers in French: A Literary History of Negritude* (Washington, D.C., 1991) by Lilyan Kesteloot is a good starting place for readers seeking more insight into this literary movement. Fitzroy Baptiste and Rupert Lewis's *Caribbean Reasonings: George Padmore, Pan-African Revolutionary* (Kingston, Jamaica, 2008) pays long-overdue attention to the life of Wright's close friend. Padmore's ideas are best summarized in his own *Pan-Africanism or Communism* (London, 1956), which was published with an introduction by Wright.

Chapter Seven: Sojourner

James T. Campbell and Kevin K. Gaines have both done important work untangling Wright's ambivalent feelings toward Africa in *Middle Passages: African American Journeys to Africa, 1787–2005* (New York, 2006) and *American Africans in Ghana* (Chapel Hill, 2006), respectively. More details about the 1955 Bandung conference that Wright attended may be found in an essay by Cary Fraser included in *Window on Freedom: Race, Civil Rights, and Foreign Affairs, 1945–1988* (Chapel Hill, 2003), edited by Brenda Gayle

Plummer. Unbeknownst to Wright, his 1955 trip to Indonesia was actually funded by the CIA. Details of CIA support for artists like Wright may be found in Frances Stonor Saunders's fascinating book *The Cultural Cold War: The CIA and the World of Arts and Letters* (New York, 1999). Readers interested in learning more about Gunnar Myrdal may consult Walter Jackson's *Gunnar Myrdal and America's Conscience: Social Engineering and Racial Liberalism, 1938–1987* (Chapel Hill, 1994). Glimpses of Wright's life in Paris may be found in the writings of many of his friends. Simone de Beauvoir's *A Transatlantic Love Affair: Letters to Nelson Algren* (New York, 1998), written in her charmingly idiosyncratic English, contains many references to de Beauvoir's friendship with the Wrights and offers details of tension in their marriage. Both volumes of Chester Himes's autobiography include colorful anecdotes about his mentor's life in Paris. See both *The Quality of Hurt: The Autobiography of Chester Himes* (New York, 1971) and *My Life of Absurdity: The Later Years* (New York, 1976). James Baldwin's ambivalent relationship with Wright during his Paris years is captured in his essay collections *Notes of a Native Son* (Boston, 1955) and *Nobody Knows My Name* (New York, 1961). Edith Anderson's *Love in Exile* (South Royalton, Vt., 1999) contains a poignant description of her brief Parisian friendship with Wright, and Oliver W. Harrington's *Why I Left America* (Jackson, Miss., 1999) offers a sketch of Wright during the last months of his life.

Index

A NOTE ON THE AUTHOR

Jennifer Jensen Wallach is assistant professor of history at the University of North Texas. She studied at the University of Arkansas, the University of Mississippi, and the University of Massachusetts, Amherst, where she received a Ph.D. in Afro-American Studies. She has also written *Closer to the Truth Than Any Fact: Memoir, Memory, and Jim Crow*. She lives with her husband in Denton, Texas.